48 ATTENTION- GETTERS

Bobetta Berthelsen, M.D.

**assisted by Lynda Nelson, M.D.
and Lourdes Morales-Gudmundsson, Ph.D.**

Pacific Press Publishing Association
Boise, Idaho
Montemorelos, Nuevo Leon, Mexico
Oshawa, Ontario, Canada

Edited by Don Mansell
Cover and book designed by Tim Larson
Type set in 10/12 Century Schoolbook

First Printing: 1986

Library of Congress Cataloging in Publication Data

Berthelsen, Bobetta.
  48 attention-getters.

  English.
  Includes indexes.
  1. Children's sermons. 2. Object-teaching.
I. Title. II. Title: Forty-eight attention-getters.
BV4315.B47 1986   252'.53   85-12060
ISBN 0-8163-0614-1

Preface

Perhaps it would be well to begin by clarifying what this book is *not*. This is not a book of stories for children. It is a book of object lessons in the form of sermonettes. The topics range from lessons dealing with Christian virtues to those that teach doctrinal truths.

But this book is principally a manual. Some sermonettes can be used as they appear in the book; others will need to be adapted to the specific resources and needs of the particular church. In other words, these object lessons are points of departure, a means of showing how common objects can become valuable teaching tools. To demonstrate how easily these sermonettes can be put together, we've included four object lessons, numbers 23, 40, 41, and 42, by Lynda Nelson, M.D., another Bella Vista mother. In the introduction of this book some simple guidelines for preparing and delivering these sermonettes are laid out.

As I was putting together these object lessons for the children of Bella Vista, Puerto Rico, it never crossed my mind that I would someday see them in print. How this came about is a witness to the guiding of the Holy Spirit.

After presenting an object lesson each week, I would receive constant encouragement and support from Lynda Nelson, who not only shared with me how her son had recalled or applied the lesson he'd learned the previous Sabbath, but who insisted that I type up the lessons so that she might have a copy.

But the idea of a book of these "sermonettes," as they were later called, was Lourdes Gudmundsson's, who, as she sat listening Sabbath after Sabbath, caught the vision of sharing this type of ministry on behalf of the younger members of God's family. Although the Holy Spirit certainly must be credited for initiating this book, it was Lourdes's insight, enthusiasm, and literary expertise that were the spark as well as the fire of this project.

It is my prayer that the same Holy Spirit that moved in the preparation of this book may guide you, as you read, to a more meaningful ministry among the children of your church.

Bobetta Berthelsen, M.D.

Dedication

This book is dedicated to those precious little ones who are made to sit quietly, but sometimes are given no place in God's worship service.

Contents

Preface

Introduction

1. Parable of the Gloves   9
2. My Atmosphere   11
3. Aloe Vera   13
4. Jewels   15
5. The Leap of Faith   17
6. A Match and Faith   21
7. Jesus Is Like a Flower   23
8. Faces in a Mirror   25
9. Weeds and Gardens   27
10. Empty Vases   29
11. Vessels   31
12. Rotten Fruit   33
13. Water of Life   35
14. Trumpets   37
15. Miriam's Leprosy   41
16. Pretty Inside   43
17. The Oyster and the Pearl   45
18. The Coral Family   47
19. Everybody Is Important   49
20. Drinking Milk   51
21. Lesson of the Candle   53
22. Hazelnuts and Trouble   55
23. The Burned Pan   57
24. Little Jobs   59
25. On Matches and Fires   61

26. Bent Seed Pods   65
27. Dirty Face   67
28. Peaches   69
29. Screws   73
30. A New Creature   75
31. Dirty Clothes   77
32. Pica Pica   79
33. Water, a Necessity   81
34. Satan   83
35. Spider Webs   85
36. Idols   87
37. Cemeteries   89
38. You Are Important   91
39. Eclipses   93
40. Squash Seed   95
41. The Penguin's Swimming Pool   97
42. The Bicyle Instruction Book   99
43. Patterns   101
44. Thanksgiving, I   103
45. Thanksgiving, II   105
46. Christmas Lights   107
47. Christmas Gifts   109
48. The Three Gifts of the Wise Men   111
Alphabetical Index   115
Subject Index   119
Index by Objects   121
Scripture Index   127

Introduction

Raising children for the Lord is a solemn and challenging task. With so many apparent failures about me, I determined to learn the secret of success. I quickly discovered that early training held the key and found my secret in an account of the childhood of Samuel. Why was it, I asked myself, that Samuel stood firm though under the direct influence of overindulgent Eli, whose own sons were failures? Samuel's mother, Hannah, had only three years to instill in him an unshakable love for God and a firm commitment to His service. How did she do it? I found her secret in the book *Patriarchs and Prophets,* page 572. "From the earliest dawn of intellect she had taught her son to love and reverence God and to regard himself as the Lord's. *By every familiar object surrounding him* she had sought to lead his thoughts up to the Creator. . . . Every day he was the subject of her prayers." Emphasis supplied.

Shortly after my discovery I was asked to tell the children's story for our worship services and decided to use familiar objects to lead the children's thoughts to God. I wish to share the lessons that I learned in leading young children's thoughts to God through familiar objects.

1. Keep your stories short. Develop only one lesson. Your effectiveness is lost after five minutes.

2. Base your stories on scripture. Parents and adults will receive a lesson too if an appropriate scripture is given for them to be pondering.

3. Always have an object to touch, see, hear, or smell. This is the key to attention and retention. The more familiar the object, the more lasting the impression will be as the child continually recalls the lesson when he views the object around his home.

4. Christ must be first as well as last in every lesson. Don't tack Him on at the end! *He* should be the reason for the story.

5. Have a helper to keep the children quiet and in order. This may not be necessary if your group is small and well disciplined, but it is a must with a large, very young group.

6. Enjoy yourself and the children. Forget the sea of adults and concentrate on getting those little faces to light up.

7. Remember that God has promised the help of every angel in heaven if you need it. With a determination to do His will and an acceptance of His promise, the victory is yours.

May these few examples be but the spark to light your imagination in leading your children's thoughts to God through familiar objects.

1
Parable of the Gloves

Scripture: Galatians 2:20.
Objects: Pair of white gloves.
Preparation: Stuff one glove with cotton to give it shape, but leave the other one empty.
Introduction for Parents and Friends: Mommies, daddies, and friends, do you ever find it hard to do the good things that you know you should do and that you really want to do? Perhaps today's lesson found in Galatians 2:20 will help you.

Sermonette:
Boys and girls, I have a glove with me. *(Put empty glove on knee.)* I'm going to have it represent you and me, Christians. Jesus wants Christians to do good things. So let's ask our glove to do something good. "Glove, please pick up the Bible so that I can read it." "Glove, please pat Eric on the cheek and let him know that I love him." The glove is not obeying. Why? Because it needs a hand in it. *(Put glove on.)* It needs some power. *(Move your fingers.)* Jesus is the hand that fits in us, and when Jesus is living inside of us, let's see what we can do. "Glove, please pick up the Bible." *(Pick up Bible with gloved hand.)* Is the glove picking the Bible up, or is the hand inside doing it? When we have Jesus inside us, He will do the good things for us. *(Take glove off.)*
Here's another glove that reminds me of many Chris-

tians. *(Put glove stuffed with cotton on knee.)* Do you suppose that this glove will do the good things Jesus wants it to? No! But look at the fingers; they're round and firm and look just as if there were a hand in them. Let's ask this glove to pick up the Bible for us. "Glove, please pick up the Bible for me." It can't. Why? It needs a hand. We said that the hand was like Jesus. Let's ask Jesus to come and fill the glove. "Jesus, this glove looks like it has a hand in it, but there's no power there. Please come in and fill it and give it life." *(Try to put your hand into filled glove.)* Jesus can't come into this glove. Why? He can come into this one. *(Put on empty glove.)* What's the difference? That's right; this glove is empty, and this one is filled with something. For Jesus to come in, we have to be empty—we have to know that we can't do anything ourselves. This little glove is still filled with self. *(Point to the stuffed glove.)* It is still trying to do good things by itself. The glove must ask Jesus to take all the self-sufficiency out of it. Let's let Jesus make this little glove empty so that it's not even pretending or trying to look like a glove filled with a hand. *(Remove stuffing.)* Now let's ask Jesus to fill the glove. *(Do.)*

Boys and girls, I want you to be like empty gloves every morning. I want you to say, "Jesus, I can't do anything good myself. Please come in and be my hand for me and do the good things that You want me to do."

Now, with Jesus' hands inside, these gloves can do all kinds of good things for Him.

2
My Atmosphere

Scripture: Acts 4:13.
Objects: Plant food; spray perfume.
Preparation: Use the most foul-smelling fish-type plant food, and make sure that each child smells it. Spray a little perfume into the air and then on each child's hand as you are talking.
Introduction for Parents and Friends: Mothers, fathers, and friends, we'd like you to ponder Acts 4:13 this morning as you consider the influence you have on your children.

Sermonette:

Boys and girls, I want you to think of somebody you love to be with. Think hard! Is that person sad and gloomy, or is he happy and cheerful? Is he selfish and wants everything his own way, or does he share and suggest doing things your way too? Is he unthoughtful and careless, or does he think about your feelings and help you? *(Allow time for responses.)*

You know, we're told that around every person there is an atmosphere, and that atmosphere either makes you want to be around that person, or makes you want to stay away from him. (See *Christ's Object Lessons*, p. 339.) Have you ever thought that you have an atmosphere around you too? Do people like to be with you, or do they not want to be around you? Let's see, I have something

11

here that we can have represent the atmosphere around you. If it were like this to be around you *(Open bottle of plant food and let children smell)*, do you think people would want to be your friends? No! Would they want to be around you? No! What kind of a person would have this kind of atmosphere around him? *(Let children answer.)* A selfish, unkind, unthoughtful person would have this type of atmosphere. That's right! I wouldn't like being around you if you were like this. You don't want to be like this.

Let's see, if you were like this would people want to be around you? *(Spray perfume into air.)* Yes! What would you be like if it was like this to be around you? A sweet, lovely, thoughtful person.

I want you to think of the kind of atmosphere that's around you. I don't want any selfish, mean, unkind children this week. I want you to be thoughtful, helpful, loving, sweet children whom everybody loves to be around.

3
Aloe Vera

Scripture: 2 Peter 1:4.
Objects: Leaf of aloe vera plant; knife; Bible.
Preparation: Bring a damp washcloth and some paper towels.
Introduction for Parents and Friends: Parents and friends, you may share in our lesson too by reading 2 Peter 1:4.

Sermonette:

What do I have in my hand? A Bible. What is the Bible? Jesus' Word. And you know, Jesus' Word is full of precious promises. What is a promise? *(Let children answer.)* That's right! The Bible is full of things that Jesus said will surely happen.

How many of you have ever had a sunburn? It hurts, doesn't it? And did you want Mommy to put something on it to make it feel better? Yes! Do you know what we use in our house? We use a special plant that Jesus made to help people when they hurt. It's the aloe vera plant. Have you ever used it? *(Show leaf.)* How do you use it? Do you just hold it like this and say, "This plant is going to make my sunburn feel better?" No! Of course not! You have to do something. First Mommy cuts the stickers off. *(Cut stickers off.)* Then she cuts the skin off, making sure that this yellow sticky stuff is off. *(Cut skin off.)* Now, do you just hold it and look at it to make your sunburn

13

better? No! What do you have to do? You have to apply it. You have to put it on you. *(Rub leaf on arm or back of hand.)* You have to rub it on carefully. And sometimes you have to put it on several times. *(Apply it several times.)* But when you do that, the aloe vera helps your sunburn feel so much better!

The promises in the Bible are kind of like the aloe vera plant. If you have a problem—Let's see, how many of you children sometimes have bad dreams or scary dreams and can't go to sleep? Have you ever had one? You don't feel good, do you? The Bible, like the aloe vera plant can make you feel better and go to sleep peacefully. But you can't just look at the Bible sitting on your shelf. What did we have to do to the aloe vera leaf? We peeled off its cover. So we have to "peel" off the cover of the Bible and get down to the insides. *(Open the Bible.)* Once we got down to the insides of the aloe vera leaf, did we just hold it? No! We had to put it on us. So it is with the Bible. We have to read what it says and then apply it to ourselves. When my children have bad dreams, we always read Jesus' promise in 2 Corinthians 10:4, 5. There it says that Jesus is so powerful that He can take our bad thoughts away from us. We ask Jesus to take those bad thoughts and dreams away from us, and then we thank Him for doing it. And does it work? Yes! When you put the aloe vera on your skin, it helps take away the hurt, and when you claim God's promise, it works too!

This next week I want you children to ask your mommies and daddies to take the peeling off the Bible and get down to the special promises God has just for you. Read those promises, and decide to believe them; they will make you feel better and live better.

4
Jewels

Scripture: Matthew 13:44.
Objects: Several pins (brooches); poster of crown jewels; Bible.
Preparation: Put Bible and pins into a small basket.
Introduction for Parents and Friends: Parents and friends, often we forget the true value of things that we take for granted. As you contemplate today's lesson in Matthew 13:44, I pray that you will determine anew to make time for God's precious promises.

Sermonette:
When I was a little girl, I liked to go to the dime store. My favorite area was the jewelry section. I liked to look at the pretty pins, earrings, and necklaces. I loved the way that they shone when the light hit them. I used to buy pretty pins, like these. *(Show.)* I liked to pretend that they were valuable, that they were real jewels, not just plastic. But I knew that they were just pretend and that they really weren't valuable, because I bought them for only fifty cents or a dollar.

Then, almost three years ago, I had the chance to see real jewels—valuable jewels—precious jewels! I went to the Tower of London to see the crown jewels. *(Show picture.)* These jewels are so beautiful, and they are the real thing. They are valuable! You can tell that they are valuable by all the guards standing around. But as I was admiring these lovely jewels with hundreds of other people, I was reminded that I had a collection of jewels even more precious than these. And I can have all the time I want to, to look at them and think about them. In fact, the longer I spend with them, the more I recognize how really valuable they are.

Do you have a collection of jewels? Yes, you do! These jewels are so precious that no money can buy them! And so valuable that they provide the means of eternal life.

What are my jewels? *(**Hold up Bible.**)* Jesus' words! Jesus' words are the most valuable jewels in the world. They can save your life forever, and nothing else can do that.

This week make sure that you spend time admiring the jewels that Jesus has given you. As you study His promises they will become even more precious.

5
The Leap of Faith

Scripture: 1 Corinthians 1:30, 31.
Objects: None.
Preparation: Choose two children, one small one and one larger. Ask two male adults to be helpers, one to stand on the other side of the church and one to stand near you.
Introduction for Parents and Friends: Mommies, daddies, and friends, many of you have thought about the "leap of faith" at one time or other, but perhaps today's lesson, found in 1 Corinthians 1:30, 31, will help you too.

Sermonette:

This morning I have chosen two helpers. *Eric (**Use the name of one of the boys**),* do you like to jump? *Shelly (**Use the name of one of the girls**),* how about you? We're going to have a jumping contest. If I asked them to jump as far as they could in one jump, would they both jump the same distance? No! Shelly would jump farther because she's older and bigger. That wouldn't be a fair contest. We already know who would win. And anybody who was little wouldn't even try to win, because he'd know that he could never jump as far as somebody bigger.

Let's see, how shall we play this game so it's fair, so everybody can win? I know. I'll do it like Jesus does our game of life. Yes! He is always fair. Does Jesus ever make mistakes? No! And He's told us that everybody can win His game.

17

OK, then, I want you both to jump from here, and whoever jumps to where *Uncle Harry* is standing (**Adult on other side of church**) in one jump will win.

Do you think you can jump that far, *Shelly?* How about you, *Eric? (**Let children try if they wish to and stay where they jumped to.**)* Who won? Nobody! Why? Because nobody jumped all that way. Do any of you think that you can jump all that way? *(**Let several others try if they think that they can.**)* Has anybody won? No! Remember that I told you that this game is just like Jesus' game of life. Why hasn't anybody won? *(**Let children answer.**)* That's right, it's impossible for any of you children to jump from here to where *Uncle Harry* is standing in one jump. But I told you that you must do it to win.

Jesus has asked us to do something impossible too. He tells us that we have to be perfect before we can go to heaven. How many of you are perfect? *(**Several small ones will always raise their hands!**)* You *think* that you're perfect, but mommy and daddy know the truth. It's interesting: if we don't know a whole lot about what Jesus requires of us, we are like you little children, and we think that we can win! We think that we can jump that far. But the older and wiser we get, the more we realize how impossible it is!

Now, in the game of life, Jesus has told us, "With men this is impossible; but with God all things are possible." Matthew 19:26. Jesus knows that you can't be perfect, and I also know that there's no way that you can jump that far. But I want to ask you a question. Can Jesus jump that far? Yes! Can Jesus live a perfect life? Yes! He did live a perfect life. And Jesus came down to this earth to be "God with us." He tells us: "Let Me live in you, and I'll live that perfect life for you. It won't be you that's doing it; it will be Me in you."

I know that *Eric* and *Shelly* can't jump that far. Nobody can jump that far! But I'll send *Uncle Vernon (**Second adult helper**)* to help you. "Uncle Vernon, if any of these children want to win, I'm going to tell them to jump up into your arms. Will you please carry them to the other side?" *(Tell him.)*

OK, *Shelly*, do you want to win? Yes! Then jump up into *Uncle Vernon's* arms. You trust him to take you to the other side. *(Do it and then repeat with smaller child, Eric.)*

How many of you children could jump all the way across in one jump now? All of you can! But can you do it by yourself? No! But you have to do *something*. You have to jump up into *Uncle Vernon's* arms. That is the "leap of faith," and you have to trust him to take you across.

This week, I want you to remember this story and jump into Jesus' arms every morning and ask Him to carry you across the day. Remember that you can't do it yourself but that He wants to do it for you; and if He does it, you'll win for sure!

6
A Match and Faith

Scriptures: Romans 12:3; 1 John 5:4.
Objects: A match; a lantern.
Preparation: Keep the match in your hand.
Introduction for Parents and Friends: Parents and friends, you may follow along with our lesson today by reading two scriptures, Romans 12:3 and 1 John 5:4.

Sermonette:
I have something in my hand. Do you think it is something big? No! It's something small, because it fits into my hand. Do you want to guess what it is? *(Let children guess.)* This is something that reminds me of what Jesus has given you and me. Let's see what it is. *(Open hand and show.)* What is it? A match! How could this match be like something that Jesus gives to you and me? How many of you have ever been kind of scared? *(Acknowledge response.)* And then something inside you said, "Jesus can take care of you. Let Jesus take care of it!" That little something is faith, and Jesus gives it to everybody. But it's like this match. I can keep it very carefully in my hand and open it up and look at it, and it's still there. *Or,* when things get dark and discouraging and I feel terrible, I can take this little match and use it. I can say, "Jesus, I am going to trust You! I'm afraid, but I'm going to remember that You can handle this situation, that You are in charge." And when I use this little match,

what happens? *(**Light the lantern.**)* Is it dark anymore? No! It's light, and I can see. This little match was no good until I used it, and then it turned the darkness into light!

That's like the faith that Jesus gives us. We can keep it very carefully, but is there any light? No! But when we use our little faith and decide, "Jesus, I'm going to trust that You are leading me, that You can take care of me," then what happens? Why, there's light.

This week, children, don't just carefully protect your faith. Use it! Let it become a big light. Decide to trust Jesus, to believe what He says.

7
Jesus Is Like a Flower

Scripture: Song of Solomon 2:1.
Objects: Sweet-smelling flowers.
Preparation: Have the flowers arranged so each child can smell them, or better yet, give each child a small blossom.
Introduction for Parents and Friends: Mothers, fathers, and friends, what a privilege we have to associate everything lovely with our Lord. Our lesson today is found in Song of Solomon 2:1.

Sermonette:

Boys and girls, Jesus is called by many different names in the Bible. He's called the Good Shepherd, the Word, the Light, the Vine, the Bread of Life. He's also called the Rose of Sharon and the Lily of the Valley.

Have you ever wondered how Jesus could be like flowers? This morning I have some pretty flowers. They aren't the rose of sharon or the lily of the valley, but they are very lovely! They are orchids.

Jesus is also very lovely. He is a lovely person. But I want you to notice something. These orchids get prettier the closer you look at them. And, what do you notice when you get real close? *(Let children smell.)* They smell lovely! Roses and lily of the valley also have lovely smells.

If I hold the orchid away from you, can you smell it? No!

Boys and girls, we must get close to Jesus and spend time with Him. Then He will be much more beautiful. Like the sweet smell from these orchids when you get close, Jesus is especially lovely when you get close to Him.

This week make Jesus a close friend—not just a God up in heaven. Talk to Him as you play. Thank Him for the sunshine when you feel it, and for the bird when you hear it singing. As you make Him your special close friend, you will find that you enjoy Him even more.

8
Faces in a Mirror

Scripture: James 1:23, 24.
Object: A mirror.
Preparation: Have some black chalk or dirt clods to streak your face with and a wet washcloth to wipe it off later.
Introduction for Parents and Friends: Mothers, fathers, and friends, daily objects can remind us of spiritual things. Please turn to James 1:23, 24 to get the most out of our lesson.

Sermonette:
Boys and girls, do you sometimes forget to study Jesus' Word? This morning I want to show you what Jesus has given us to remind us every morning to study His Word. What could it be? *(Show mirror.)* A mirror! How does a mirror remind us to study Jesus' Word? Well, Jesus tells us that His Word is like a mirror.

Does your mommy or daddy ever leave the house in the morning without looking into the mirror first? No! Why do they look into the mirror? *(Let children answer.)* That's right! They want to make sure that their hair is combed, that their face is clean, and that they look OK. You know, that is what Jesus' Word is for, to show us where we're messed up, what needs cleaning or combing.

What if you looked into the mirror and saw a face like this? *(Make an angry face and look into the mirror*

25

and then at the children.) Jesus' Word tells us how terrible angry faces really are. It says that it's better to live in the desert than with an angry person and that an angry face outside means the heart of a murderer inside.

What if you looked into the mirror and saw a face like this? *(Put several dirty smudges on your face.)* Again Jesus' Word tells us that we should be orderly, clean, and decent.

The mirror never fools you. You can decide, "I'm not going to pay any attention to what the mirror says." But that doesn't make you look any better. You still look the same. And boys and girls, Jesus' Word never lies either. It always shows us where we're messed up. And like the mirror, we must look at it every day so we can see our problems and then ask Jesus to take care of those problems.

Tomorrow morning, when you look into the mirror, ask yourself, "Did I remember to look into Jesus' Word this morning?"

9
Weeds and Gardens

Scripture: Proverbs 29:15.
Objects: Picture of vegetables; picture of a garden; three weeds.
Preparation: Have the three weeds of varying size, the smallest one quite small and the largest as big as you can find.
Introduction for Parents and Friends: Mommies, daddies, and friends, training young characters is not an easy task, and it's often easier to turn your head, but perhaps our lesson found in Proverbs 29:15 will help you take courage.

Sermonette:

What are these? *(Show picture of vegetables.)* Vegetables. Where do they come from? *(Show picture of a garden.)* A garden. You know, our family used to have a vegetable garden just like this. It was so pretty. We got tomatoes, beans, cucumbers, and lettuce from it.

Taking care of that garden reminded me of caring for the character gardens that Jesus gives mommies and daddies. Did you know that each one of you is a character garden? Jesus asks your mommies and daddies to work carefully with your character gardens so that your character will grow lovely "vegetables"—like kindness, obedience, cheerfulness, and unselfishness. These are the lovely vegetables in a character garden.

But sometimes your character gardens get like our vegetable garden did. We got too busy. We were doing good things—working at the hospital, doing church activities—but we just didn't make time to work in the garden. What started to happen in the garden? Something else began growing besides the vegetables. Weeds!

At first they were very little. *(Show little weed.)* It wouldn't have taken too much work to pull them out. But we didn't take the time right then, and what happened to those little weeds? They grew! *(Show medium weed.)* Now the weeds were even bigger, and you could hardly see the vegetables, but we still could have pulled the weeds out. It would have taken more work though, but we just didn't take the time.

Not too long after that, our vegetable garden was a complete mess! You couldn't find any vegetables. Why? The weeds were so big and so thick that they crowded out all the vegetables. *(Show huge weed.)*

Boys and girls, when your mommies and daddies take time to spank you and punish you, don't get mad at them. Remember, they are taking time to pull the weeds out of your character garden. If you have the weed of complaining or pouting, and your mommy and daddy don't take time to pull that weed, it will eventually grow into a huge weed, and then it will be very hard to dig out. But when they take time now, you will always be a lovely garden that people want to be around.

10
Empty Vases

Scripture: Ephesians 3:17-19.
Objects: Two opaque flower vases; bouquet of flowers.
Preparation: Leave one vase empty, but fill the other one with pieces of gum paper, candy wrappers, pictures of cars, toys, clothes.
Introduction for Parents and Friends: Mothers, fathers, and friends, often we complain that God isn't filling us with His love like we think He should, but perhaps we are too full of self for Him to fill. Please turn to Ephesians 3:17-19 and follow along with our lesson.

Sermonette:
Boys and girls, I have a lovely bouquet of flowers. *(Show.)* I wonder which vase I should put them in. They would look pretty in either vase. How can I decide which vase to put them in? Shall we put them into this one? *(Try putting flowers into filled vase.)* What's wrong? *(Look inside vase, show to children, and let one of them start pulling things out.)* My! This vase is filled with all sorts of junk! *(Continue to pull things out slowly.)* Can I put these beautiful flowers into this vase if it is full of junk? No! But this one is empty, so I can easily use it. *(Put flowers into empty vase.)*

Boys and girls, you are like these pretty vases. Jesus wants to fill you with a bouquet of flowers to make your life sweet. *(Smell flowers.)* But what does Jesus need before He can fill you like He wants to? That's right! You have to be empty. This vase is full of junk! Do you suppose that your life could be filled with some of these things? *(Take out bits of things.)* Let's see, here are some clothes, food, toys, music, selfishness. What do I have to do before I can use this vase? I have to get rid of all the junk. And that's exactly what Jesus must do before He can use you as He wants to. He has to pull out all this junk, so that there is room for some flowers. *(Put a few flowers from the other vase into this one.)* Jesus can use any container, but it must be empty, or He can't fill it with His love. Maybe this vase thought it looked pretty with all this junk inside it, but doesn't it look much better with the flowers?

You know, we may think that what we're filled with is important and pretty—thoughts of clothes, toys, TV, cars, and so on—but if we let Jesus get rid of all those things from our lives, He'll fill us with real beauty, like these lovely flowers.

This next week, when you see a vase filled with pretty flowers, remember to let Jesus get rid of the junk in your life and fill you with the beautiful flowers of His love.

11
Vessels

Scripture: 2 Timothy 2:20, 21.
Objects: Two vases of different colors; set of measuring cups; kettle; tray.
Preparation: Put all the containers into a basket.
Introduction for Parents and Friends: Mommies, daddies, and friends, you may follow our lesson by reading along in 2 Timothy 2:20, 21.

Sermonette:
I have some things in my basket that remind me of you boys and girls, and of your mommies and daddies. Shall we see what they are? *(Have children take things out and place them on a tray, identifying each thing as it is taken out.)*

Now, look at all these containers! The Bible talks about containers, only it calls them "vessels." You know what it says about these vessels? It says that *Eric, Shelly,* and your mommies and daddies are just like these vessels. Jesus wants you to be empty like these so He can fill you up with His love and use you.

Let's start with these vessels. What are they? Flower vases. What color are they? Black and white. *(Whatever color you have.)* Which vase is the most useful? Both! Boys and girls, Jesus can use you no matter what color you are!

What are these? *(Hold up measuring cups.)* They are

measuring cups. If your mommy were going to make some bread or some biscuits, which measuring cup would be the most important, the big one or the little ones? She uses them all, doesn't she! Boys and girls, it doesn't make any difference whether we are big or little. Jesus needs *all* of us! Your mommies and daddies are big and you are little, but just like mommy needs the little measuring cup, Jesus needs you little children.

There is one more container left. The kettle. *(Hold up the kettle.)* Have you ever wished that you were somebody else? That you were someone more important? What if the kettle wished that he could be pretty like this vase? Can I use a pretty vase to cook beans in? No! Boys and girls, Jesus made you just like you are for a very special reason. He has a special purpose for your life. He doesn't want us all to be pretty vases! He needs some kettles and some measuring cups. Don't try to be like somebody else. Thank Jesus that He made you just like you are, because He especially needed you.

12
Rotten Fruit

Scripture: 1 Samuel 16:7.
Objects: Two apples, knife, cutting board.
Preparation: Choose one beautiful-looking apple that you know has worms inside and one ugly-looking apple that is good inside.
Introduction for Parents and Friends: Mothers, fathers, and friends, choosing friends can be very difficult, but God's advice in our lesson today is worth remembering. Please turn to 1 Samuel 16:7.

Sermonette:

Boys and girls, we have an apple tree in our back yard, and the apples are beginning to ripen. I brought a couple of them to show you today. *(Show the two apples.)* If you could eat one of these apples right now, which one would you choose? *(Let several children answer.)* Why are you all choosing the pretty apple? *(Let them answer.)* Remember, Jesus made the apple to be sweet and good to eat. He didn't necessarily make it to look beautiful. Does anybody else want to choose? I know that this apple doesn't look very attractive on the outside, but does that mean that it's bad on the inside too?

Shall we cut the apples open? Let's cut the pretty one, the one that you chose first. *(Cut open.)* Ugh! Do you still want to eat this one? *(Show the worms.)* No! You know, Jesus is not fooled by what's on the outside. He goes by what's on the

33

inside. Let's cut the ugly apple. *(Cut open.)* Wow! How about a bite of this one!

Boys and girls, people are like these apples. Jesus says, "Don't choose your friends by how pretty they are. It's what they are like inside that really matters." People who are not very attractive on the outside are sometimes the kindest, most thoughtful people on the inside.

Next time you meet somebody new, remember it's not their looks that is important, but what kind of a person they are.

13
Water of Life

Scripture: Isaiah 59:1, 2.

Objects: Dying plant; glass of water; slips of paper with promises on them; small piece of cardboard with UNBE-LIEF printed on it.

Preparation: Slip the cardboard over the mouth of the glass and quickly turn it upside down. The cardboard will keep the water from running out. Do this several times at home to make sure that you can do it right.

Introduction for Parents and Friends: Mothers, fathers, and friends, why is it that we do not enjoy God's promises more? Perhaps today's lesson from Isaiah 59:1, 2 will give us a clue.

Sermonette:

Boys and girls, I brought something very special to show you. It's one of my favorite plants. *(Show dying plant.)* What's the matter? Don't you like my plant? Well, I know that it looks awful, but that shouldn't make any difference! Or should it? Why does my plant look so awful? It used to be so beautiful. *(Let child answer.)* It's dying? Why do you think that it's dying? Oh, but I water my plant every day. Let me show you. *(Reach for glass of water.)*

You know, this little plant reminds me of you and me. Jesus is the water of life *(Show glass of water)*, and He promises life to us freely. Let's read some of these promises. *(Place slips of paper into the glass of water after reading them.)*

1. "This is the promise that he hath promised us, even eternal life." 1 John 2:25.

2. "Beloved, *now* are we the sons of God." 1 John 3:2. Emphasis supplied.

3. "If any of you lack wisdom, let him ask of God . . . and it shall be given him." James 1:5.

4. "I will never leave you nor forsake you." Hebrews 13:5, NKJV.

These special promises are for us. They are like water to my dying plant. But now how do we use these promises? How do I water my plant? Let me show you.

First I put this cardboard over the top of the glass, to keep the water from spilling all over, and then I water my plant. *(Do.)* What's wrong? Well I'm watering my plant, am I not? I water it every day like this! *(Someone will mention the cardboard.)* You think that the cardboard has something to do with my plant dying? Let's see. *(Turn glass back over and remove cardboard.)* It has something written on it. *(Show.)* UNBELIEF. Boys and girls, do you suppose that you may be dying just like my special plant, because the cardboard of unbelief is keeping God's promises away from you? Let's get unbelief out of the way. *(Pour the water on the plant.)* That's much better! Why didn't I do that sooner?

Boys and girls, maybe you should remove the unbelief from your promises too so that Jesus' water of life can get to you.

14
Trumpets

Scripture: 1 Corinthians 10:11, 12.
Objects: Picture of orderly tents of Israel; tabernacle with cloud; picture of a family; trumpet.
Preparation: Use felt tabernacle and cloud of God's presence from the felt set on a small felt board. Have somebody behind the platform play a call on the trumpet at the appropriate times. Have the trumpeter, if a parent, come out on the last call and give his or her testimony.
Introduction for Parents and Friends: Mothers, fathers, and friends, the methods used by God for leading the children of Israel may be different from the methods He uses with us, but the importance of obedience is just the same, as you will discover in our lesson text in 1 Corinthians 10:11, 12.

Sermonette:
God had just delivered His special people, the Israelites, from Egypt. What a huge crowd of people they were! He gave special instructions to their leader, Moses. He told Moses how to organize them and discipline them into a mighty army. *(Show picture of tents.)* He had Moses divide the people into smaller companies with a head officer for each company. Then He had Moses instruct the head officers very carefully in what God wanted His people to do. He also told the head officers to

tell their companies how important it was to obey God's instructions and do just what He wanted them to do. The head officers then went back and instructed their companies.

When it came time for God's special people to travel on, God gave instructions very clearly to everyone at the same time so that they would move together in an orderly way. How would you do that if you were God? His people didn't have TVs or radios or walkie-talkies so that Moses could tell everybody at the same time. How do you think God told everyone at the same time? What did He use?

When the time came for His people to move forward, the cloud over the tabernacle lifted up. *(Show on felt board.)* Then two priests came out of the tabernacle and gave a signal that everybody could hear. *(Trumpet plays.)*

Did you hear that? Did the people in the back of the church hear it? What did it mean? I don't know, but God's special people knew because their head officers had instructed them very carefully.

Let's pretend that you are in one of those companies. One morning you see the cloud lifted up. *(Show on felt board.)* "Oh, Mommy, God is going to give us some special instructions. We've got to listen carefully." And just then you hear the trumpet speaking. *(Trumpet plays.)* "Mommy, I remember what that signal means. It means everybody pay attention." And so you drop everything that you are doing and listened carefully. *(Trumpet plays different tune.)*

"What does that message mean? Do you remember?" And mother would say, "That means that we must take down our tent." Do you suppose that you would run and play after hearing that message? No! You remember that the chief officer told you how important it was to obey God's instructions. So you start packing too!

(Trumpet plays different tune.) "Oh, I'm so glad we've finished, Mother. That message means that we're to get into line to start moving."

But what if you decided not to learn what the messages meant, or what if you decided not to do what they said? What would happen? You would displease God! That's right!

Remember, we're God's special people too. I'd like to think that each family is a company. *(Show picture of family.)* Who is the head officer? Usually Father. Does God want us to all work and move together today in an orderly way? Yes! Does He use trumpets to give us the messages? What do you think? Did you hear a trumpet this morning telling you that it was time for church? *(Trumpeter comes out and blows trumpet.)* Let's ask a head officer. "Head officer, how do you get instructions from God? Does He blow this trumpet at your house?"

(Trumpeter or other parent answers.) "Our trumpet today is the Bible, and as head officer I'm to instruct my company in God's will."

Children, this next week, as your head officer gives you God's special instructions, don't say, "Oh, why do we have to do that! Why can't we go there?" Remember, it is important for us to obey God's instructions.

15
Miriam's Leprosy

Scripture: James 4:11.
Objects: Picture of an elderly woman; picture of tabernacle; picture of cloud of the presence.
Preparation: Place the tabernacle and cloud from the felt set on a small felt board.
Introduction for Parents and Friends: Mothers, fathers, and friends, please open your Bibles to James 4:11. Our lesson today is quite specific about criticizing our leaders.

Sermonette:
Miriam was an elderly woman. She was more than 90 years old, old enough to be a grandma. *(Show picture.)* She was respected and honored by all the camp of Israel, just as you respect and honor your grandma. In fact, Miriam was one of the three leaders especially chosen by God. She was a prophetess; in other words, God spoke to the people through her. See Micah 6:4.

But Miriam became jealous that her "little brother," Moses, was making decisions without asking for her advice. So you know what she did? She went to her brother Aaron and started whispering about Moses. "I don't like the wife that Moses chose. She has darker skin than we have," she whispered. Was Miriam saying kind words about Moses? No! Miriam was criticizing God's chosen leader. I know that Moses was her brother, and I know

41

that she was old enough to be a grandma, but she was saying unkind things about God's chosen leader.

Do you ever say unkind things about the leaders God has put over you? Do you ever get upset and say unkind things about your mommy or daddy? Or, what about your teacher at school? Does she make you angry sometimes? Or your Sabbath School teachers? Do you sometimes complain that their programs are boring? Your mommies and daddies, your school teachers, and your Sabbath School teachers are church leaders like Moses.

How does God feel when we say unkind things about His leaders? Do you know? Did God do anything to Miriam for criticizing her brother? I'll say He did! He called Miriam and Aaron and Moses to His special tabernacle tent. *(Show on felt board.)* His cloud was over the tabernacle showing that God was there. God spoke to them and said, "How can you say these unkind things against My special leader, Moses?" And then the cloud left the tabernacle. *(Remove cloud.)* This showed that God was angry. And all of a sudden Aaron cried out, "Miriam, look at you!" And when Miriam looked at herself, do you know what she saw? She was white all over! She had a terrible disease called leprosy!

What happened to people when they became leprous? They had to go outside the camp and tell everyone, "I am unclean! unclean!"

Why did Miriam get leprosy? Because she was saying unkind things about God's chosen leader.

Does God want us to say unkind things about our leaders—our mommy, daddy, or teachers? No! When we complain and say unkind things against them, we are really saying unkind things against God.

Wouldn't it be nice if this coming week your friends heard only kind things from your lips?—no complaints about your parents or teachers, the leaders that God has given to you?

16
Pretty Inside

Scripture: Matthew 12:34, 35.
Objects: Silver pitcher with dirt clod and water; four clear glasses; tray; large spoon.
Preparation: Dissolve enough dirt to make the water muddy, but have a lump of clayey dirt in the bottom that can be removed with large spoon. Set glasses on small tray.
Introduction for Parents and Friends: Mommies, daddies, and friends, our lesson today, found in Matthew 12:34, 35, explains why there are so many foul-mouthed people in our world today.

Sermonette:

Isn't this a pretty pitcher? It reminds me of you children. You're so pretty and neat and tidy for Sabbath. Would you like a drink from my pitcher? *(Pour into first glass.)* Ugh! Do you want to drink this? No! But the pitcher looks so good, doesn't it?

You know, your teachers and friends are looking at your outside, and it looks so nice and clean and lovely, but what happens when you open your mouth? What comes out? Are your words thoughtful, kind, and happy words, or *(Pour into second glass)* are they grumpy, mean, sassy words?

This pitcher has decided that he wants only clean water to come out of his mouth. Let's see. *(Pour into third glass.)* Ugh! It's still dirty. How can the pitcher make clean, tasty water come out? How can you get thoughtful, happy words to come out of your mouth? *(Pour into fourth glass.)* Well, somebody else has to come and clean this pitcher out. *(Use spoon and remove the clod of dirt.)* How can this pitcher expect to have clean water come out of his mouth when this yucky dirt clod was inside it?

Boys and girls, you have to have someone clean the yucky selfishness out of your mind before your mouth will say kind and thoughtful things. The pitcher can't clean itself out. And neither can you clean your mind. Who makes your mind clean? Jesus. Do you remember the text that says, "A new heart also will I give you"? Jesus is talking about your mind. He wants to give you a new, clean mind.

Boys and girls, I love to see you so clean on the outside. But are you as clean on the inside? Jesus will clean you, if you ask Him to, but you must want Him to every day. If you don't, Satan will put a clump of yucky dirt back into your mind.

This next week, ask Jesus every morning to make your mind clean and to keep it clean. OK?

17
The Oyster and the Pearl

Scripture: Romans 8:28.
Objects: Oyster shell; small stone; pearl.
Introduction for Parents and Friends: Mothers, fathers, and friends, please follow our lesson today found in Romans 8:28, and perhaps you will learn to look at your little irritations differently.

Sermonette:

Boys and girls, today Jesus has a special lesson for you from one of His animals. What animal lived inside this? *(Show oyster shell.)* An oyster, that's right! Where do oysters live? In the sea. Do they live in houses like we live in? No. Jesus gave the oyster a shell to live in. See how hard it is! *(Show.)* When an oyster is in danger, he closes the shell quickly for protection. But sometimes a little piece of stone gets into his shell *(Put stone into shell)*, like this. How do you think that makes the oyster feel? Have you ever had a stone in your shoe? It hurts. Well, this stone doesn't feel good to the soft little oyster either! But do you think he murmurs and complains and grumbles about it? No! Jesus has given him a way to take care of his trouble.

Jesus has promised that whatever comes to us, even terrible trouble, He can turn it into something for our good, if we let Him.

Would you like to know what Jesus does for the little

45

oyster? Do you think He takes the stone out? No! He starts covering the ugly little stone with some soft secretions that smooth the rough edges. Gradually the sharp corners of the stone are covered and made smooth. Then He changes the ugly, dirty color of the stone into lovely colors like a rainbow. *(Show pearl.)* Isn't this a beautiful jewel? What's it called? A pearl. Yes! But what was it when it started out? A stone. The stone got through the protecting shell and began to hurt the oyster. But Jesus changed that trouble into a beautiful jewel. Isn't it wonderful what Jesus can do for an oyster?

Boys and girls, has Jesus given you a protective shell? Yes, but it's not like the oyster's. Jesus has His angels around you. But sometimes Jesus lets trouble like a stone come in. Have you ever had trouble come to you? Little troubles are like little stones in your shoes. They don't feel good. What do you do when trouble comes to you? Do you grumble and complain and say that Jesus doesn't love you anymore? Does the oyster grumble and complain and get mad at Jesus? No! Who do you suppose is more special to Jesus, you or the oyster? If Jesus can change the little piece of stone, the little irritating trouble of the oyster into a lovely pearl, don't you think He will do the same for you? Surely He will! He promises that "all things work together for good!" But in order to turn a stone into a pearl, you have to let Jesus do it His way.

This next week, I want you to remember the little oyster, and when a little trouble comes to you, don't complain and get upset. Take it to Jesus and let Him make a pearl out of it.

18
The Coral Family

Scripture: Colossians 3:18-21.
Objects: Picture of a family; close-up picture of coral polyps; several large coral pieces; small coral pieces.
Preparation: Have many small pieces of coral to give to children.
Introduction for Parents and Friends: Mothers, fathers, and friends, you may follow along with our lesson by reading Colossians 3:18-21.

Sermonette:
Jesus is *so* thoughtful! He carefully plans everything to make us happy. He has given each one of you something very special. How many of you children are part of a family? *(Acknowledge their hands.)* What is a family? *(Let several answer.)* A family is made up of several people. *(Show picture.)* Usually there is a mommy, a daddy, and some children, but not always. Sometimes there isn't a mommy or a daddy. Sometimes a family is made up of children who live with a grandparent, or children who have been adopted by adults.

What is it that makes these people a family? What is special about a family? You know, Jesus has given you your family. He has also given you things in nature to teach you about your family.

Does anybody know what this is? *(Show close-up picture of coral polyps.)* This is a picture of some coral.

Can you see the little "people" of this piece of coral? *(Point them out.)* I have a piece of real coral here, and I want you to look at it very carefully to see if you can find the little window that belongs to each member of this coral family. *(Show large corals.)* Look closely. Do you see the little window? *(Point out several.)*

If each little animal in this coral family didn't do his job and keep up his room, there wouldn't be any coral. One little animal by himself can't make a pretty piece of coral. Each one of the little animals has to do his part. They have to work together. They are like your family. A daddy by himself is not a family. A mommy by herself cannot make a family. Children by themselves are not a family. When a mommy and a daddy and children work together, they make a whole family.

Are you children doing your part in your family? Do you take care of your room, pick up your toys, and put your clothes away and do your part like these little coral animals do? I'm going to give each one of you a piece of coral. I want you to remember that your family is like this piece of coral. Unless each one does his little part, there is no real family. A whole family is a mommy and a daddy and children who work together.

Jesus wants you to do your part in your family just like the coral. OK?

19
Everybody Is Important

Scripture: Romans 12:4, 5.
Objects: Large paper doll; scissors.
Preparation: A large paper figure used for bulletin boards is best.
Introduction to Parents and Friends: Mommies, daddies, and friends, if you've ever had second thoughts about bringing your little ones to church, please share our lesson with us by meditating on Romans 12:4, 5.

Sermonette:

Let's see the hands of everybody who came to church today. *(Acknowledge hands.)* Did your mommies and daddies come to church too? I want to ask you, since you children are so little, do you suppose that Jesus would miss you if you didn't come to church? How important are you, *Eric, Shelly, Timmy,* to Jesus?

Some grown-ups may think that little children are a bother in church, that they shouldn't be here. But that's not the way Jesus sees it. Jesus tells us that all of us are like parts of a body. Jesus' church is this body. Some of us are fingers, others are eyes, but if you didn't have a finger or an eye, your body wouldn't be complete! Let me show you how important you are to Jesus and why He misses you if you don't come to church.

This paper doll's name is Paul. He's just a boy doll, but I'm going to use him to represent Jesus' church today. *(Show the doll.)*

Let's see, there is *Shelly*. She's not very big is she? Can you think of some part of your body that's not very big? How about the thumb? Let's pretend that *Shelly* is just a little thumb. Suppose her Mommy and Daddy didn't think that it was important enough to bring her to church and Sabbath School. You know how Jesus would feel? His thumb would be missing. *(Cut the thumb off the doll.)* Can you pick up things without your thumb? *(Show, holding thumb in palm of hand.)* No! He would really miss *Shelly* if she weren't here, wouldn't He?

Eric, you and *Timmy* aren't very big either. I can think of something else that isn't very big. How about your eyes? If you didn't have any eyes, you would still live, wouldn't you? But if *Eric* and *Timmy* weren't included in Jesus' church, He would surely miss them. *(Cut the eyes out of the doll.)* Close your eyes tightly. It would be like being blind with both eyes missing.

Johnny is a little bigger. We'll have him be a leg. *Johnny*, do you suppose Jesus would miss you if you weren't here? *(Cut one leg off the doll.)* Can Paul walk very well with one leg missing? No!

Do you see what I'm trying to show you? Paul started out being a lovely little boy, but look at him now. You children may be little, like little fingers, eyes, and mouth, but when you aren't included, Jesus misses you just as Paul misses his fingers or eyes.

I want you to always remember that your size is not what makes you important to Jesus. Jesus needs the big people, but He needs you little people too. If you aren't here, He misses you, just like Paul misses his fingers and eyes.

20
Drinking Milk

Scripture: 1 Peter 2:2.
Objects: Newborn baby; baby bottle.
Preparation: Take the baby up with you.
Introduction for Parents and Friends: Mothers, fathers, and friends, you may follow our lesson by reading 1 Peter 2:2.

Sermonette:

How many of you have babies at your house? *(Acknowledge their hands and hold the baby so they can see him.)* What does a baby do if he is hungry? Yes, he cries! Is it just a little cry? No, he really cries, if Mommy doesn't get the bottle right away! *(Show the bottle.)* But once you give him the bottle, he becomes happy and content. He really guzzles the milk.

This little baby reminds me of Jesus' little children. Who are Jesus' little children? You are! And you know, Jesus wants to feed you, just as Mommy feeds the baby. He says that you need to drink the milk of His Word, so that you can grow up to be like Him.

Jesus has a special place where He gives little children the milk of His Word. Do you know where that is? It is in your own special Sabbath School! Jesus is happy when your mommies and daddies bring you to Sabbath School on time. They know how important it is that you drink all of Jesus' good Bible milk. They know that if they get you here late, you wouldn't get all the Bible milk that Jesus had for you. If this little baby doesn't get enough milk, what happens to him? He cries and cries, and he can't grow up. You would get that way too, if you don't get to drink all the special Bible milk that Jesus has for you in Sabbath School.

You know, next Sabbath, I'd like you to make it easier for your mommies and daddies to get you to Sabbath School on time. You could eat your breakfast quickly and carefully. Maybe you could dress yourself. You could make sure that you didn't get dirty after you got dressed, and you older children could get up a little earlier and be all ready so Mom and Dad wouldn't have to wait for you. Now that you can see how important it is for you to be at Sabbath School on time, why don't you try to make it easier for Mommy and Daddy next Sabbath.

21
Lesson of the Candle

Scripture: Isaiah 55:8, 9.
Objects: Candle; funnel; matches; Bible.
Preparation: Use a large funnel and choose larger children first. Have the child hold the funnel upside down by the funnel tip.
Introduction for Parents and Friends: Mothers, fathers, and friends, although we must show authority and leadership, there is a time to say, "I cannot do it." Perhaps our lesson from Isaiah 55:8, 9 will help you recognize this fact.

Sermonette:
How many of you want to be in heaven someday? *(Recognize hands.)* But you know, we're told that the people who live in heaven will be very special people. Will they be selfish? No! Will they be disobedient? No! Will they be mean and angry? No! Jesus tells us that if we want to be in heaven someday, we have to become that special kind of person right now! What has Jesus given us to make us that kind of person? *(Hold up Bible.)* His Word! That's right.

I have a funrel, and I'm going to pretend that this is the Bible, Jesus' Word. I also have a candle. *(Light the candle.)* I'm going to pretend that becoming the kind of person that will be in heaven is like blowing the candle out. Jesus has given us His Word *(Hold up the funnel)* to make us ready for heaven. *(Point to candle.)* With His Word our lives are to be changed. This funnel is supposed to change the candle. With it you can blow out the candle.

Who would like to use the funnel to blow the candle out for me? *(Let a child try blowing through the narrow end of the funnel.)* What's wrong? You know, this is just like it is in life. Many people have the Bible in their hands *(Hold up the funnel)*, but we don't see a changed life. The candle burns just the same as before. Some people get discouraged and say, "This doesn't work! It's impossible! I can't have a changed life!"

Well, boys and girls, when you use Jesus' Word to change your life *(Hold up the funnel)*, you must use it His way, not your way! When you've been blowing into this funnel, you've been blowing into the little end—because you can get your mouth around it. But Jesus says, "Blow into the big end." But you say, "I can't get my mouth around the big end! *(Show.)* It's impossible, Jesus!" That's like saying, "I've got to do it my way—it makes more sense that way." Maybe blowing on the little end makes more sense to us, but it doesn't work.

Who would like to use Jesus' Word, the funnel, the way He says it should be used? *(Choose a little child to blow into the big end aiming the little end at the candle.)* See if you can blow the candle out? See if we get a changed life. See how simple it is?

Boys and girls, Jesus wants us always to do things His way, even though sometimes it doesn't seem to make sense, because His way always works. Our lives will be changed when we use Jesus' Word His way.

22
Hazelnuts and Trouble

Scripture: 1 Peter 2:9.
Objects: Jar with beans and several hazelnuts.
Preparation: Use a large jar and test it several times to make sure that you can shake the nuts to the top.
Introduction for Parents and Friends: Parents and friends, what is your attitude toward being different? Please share our lesson with us by reading 1 Peter 2:9.

Sermonette:
Some days are wet and dreary. On such days some people feel sad, discouraged, and low. But you don't even have to have that kind of a day to feel "blue." How many of you had problems last week? How many of you had trials, like hardships, things that could make you feel so discouraged you felt like giving up?

Let's see if we can think of some examples. Maybe you overheard a friend saying some unkind things about you. Maybe your special friend decided to sit with somebody else in Sabbath School today instead of with you. Maybe you were punished and you didn't think that it was fair. You know, Jesus lets these troubles come to us, and Satan tries to use them to make us discouraged and blue. Jesus has promised that if we let Him, He'll keep us from getting down and discouraged. He can use these problems to make us better persons.

You've all been looking at this jar of beans, haven't

you? *(Show jar.)* What do they have to do with troubles? I want you to look at this jar of beans *very* carefully. All the beans are just alike—or are they? Do you see something in here that doesn't look like a bean?

Yes, there are some oddballs in this bunch. In fact, they look like "nuts." You know, Jesus has told us that He wants us to be different from the rest of the bunch. We're "special." Some people may think that we're "nuts," but we're *very* special. If we let Jesus take our bumps and problems and troubles, He can keep us from getting "down" and discouraged.

I'm going to let you bump this jar around—give it some trials and troubles—and let's see what happens to those people who trust in Jesus. Let's see if they get down and discouraged, or if Jesus keeps them on top—happy, optimistic, cheerful—no matter how hard they get bumped. *(Let children bump jar around until the nuts come to the top.)*

What happened to Jesus' special nuts? They're on top. They may have gotten bumped around a lot and even gotten hurt, but they are not down and discouraged like everybody else.

Boys and girls, let Jesus make you special this week. Let Him keep you from getting discouraged and blue when you get bumped around, OK?

23
The Burned Pan

Scripture: Psalm 55:16, 17.
Objects: Pan with scorched food (black all over inside) and its lid; pan and lid which are bright and shiny.
Preparation: None.
Introduction for Parents and Friends: Mothers, fathers, and friends, we invite you to share with us in the study of our lesson found in Psalm 55:16, 17.

Sermonette:
How many of you like breakfast? *(Acknowledge hands.)* Every morning somebody gets up and cooks something that smells so good on the stove! Well, that's what I did one morning this week. I put something on the stove to cook. *(Give pan to a child to hold on outstretched arms like a stove.)* And while it was cooking, the baby cried and needed a change of diapers. Then big brother called for help in making his bed, and I saw some things which needed to be picked up in the living room. Now, all of these things that I stopped to do were good things—important things—but what was most important? That's right, the pan on the hot stove burner. Pretty soon we smelled something that didn't smell like good breakfast smells, and we saw some smoke. What do you think I found when I opened the lid to that pan? *(Take pan off "stove" and open lid to show children.)* Ugh! Black ugly burn marks! And the food certainly was not fit to eat.

This ugly black pan reminds me of you and me—our lives. Who fills our lives with ugly thoughts? That's right, it's Satan. The boy who hits little sister, the girl who always whines and fusses, the child who always wants to have his way—these are lives that look like this pan. *(Show burned pan.)* Do you want your life like this pan—full of angry, ugly thoughts and actions? It doesn't have to be. Who can keep you happy and shining, doing kind deeds and thinking good thoughts—like this pan? *(Show shiny, clean pan.)* That's right, it's Jesus. But we must ask Him to do it in us. We must ask Him into our lives. We must not let ourselves get so busy doing other things, even good and important things, that we forget to ask Him to help us. In the morning, before you eat breakfast or before you take your toys out, ask Jesus to make you happy and shining. At school, ask Him to keep you bright. Before you go to town with mommy, talk to Him again. *All* day, *every* day, you must talk to Jesus about keeping you shining, just like I have to watch my pan every day, all the time, if I don't want it to burn.

This week I want you to remember my two pans *(Show two pans)*, and each morning, before anything else, ask Jesus to keep you shining for Him.

24
Little Jobs

Scripture: Colossians 3:23.
Objects: Bible, surgical mask; a cluster of hydrangea blossoms.
Preparation: Keep the hydrangea blossoms in a sack.
Introduction for Parents and Friends: Parents and friends, if you've ever wished for a more rewarding job, please follow along with our lesson today from Colossians 3:23.

Sermonette:
How many of you want to be a great preacher or missionary when you grow up and preach great sermons like Peter and Paul did, or like Pastor *(Name of your church pastor)*? *(Hold up Bible.)* That's an important job. Or, how many of you want to be surgeons when you grow up *(Put on surgical mask)* and fix people's legs so they can walk or take out cataracts so people can see? Are those important jobs? Yes! But you aren't a preacher now, and you aren't a doctor now. What *can* you do that is important?

Do you think that picking up your toys is a great, important job? Do you do it carefully, the way the pastor plans his sermons? And how about making your bed? Is that such an important job that you never, never forget to do it?

Boys and girls, Jesus tells us that every time you faithfully pick up your toys or make the bed, it's just as important a job as preaching a great sermon or doing difficult surgery.

Jesus has given you something to help remind you of how important your little jobs are. What do I have in my hand? *(Pull off a single hydrangea blossom and hold up.)* A flower! Is this hydrangea blossom a very big flower? No! It's a small flower. Let it represent picking up your toys. *(Hold up cluster of hydrangea blossoms.)* Each little flower is like the little things that you do each day. When you pick up your toys faithfully every day and make your bed every day—just little things—Jesus knows about it even if everybody else doesn't know. You look lovely and your life smells sweet, like a helpful, obedient child.

I'm going to give you each a hydrangea blossom, and you may show your mommy and daddy. These blossoms are like the little things that you do each day. They add up to make a lovely smell and a beautiful sight. Remember, Jesus knows that your little jobs are just as important as the doctor's or preacher's jobs.

25
On Matches and Fires

Scripture: Matthew 5:14, 16.
Objects: Potatoes and corn on the cob wrapped in foil; a little kindling wood and paper; matchbox without rough striking surface; matchbox with rough striking surface; Bible.
Preparation: Have some potatoes and corn already wrapped in foil. Have two not wrapped, so the children can see you wrap them. A lot of wood and paper is not necessary, but have enough to look realistic.
Introduction for Parents and Friends: Mothers, fathers, and friends, if Jesus' requests of you often seem hard, perhaps today's lesson from Matthew 5:14, 16 will encourage you.

Sermonette:
Last week we went camping at El Faro. We hadn't been there very long when we started getting hungry. I had brought something very special for supper *(Show potatoes and corn)*—potatoes and corn on the cob! They were all wrapped in foil. *(Wrap the two.)* But what needed to be done? They needed to be cooked. So I asked Brad if he would please start a bonfire.

First he scooped out the sand to make a pit *(Go through motions)*; then he put down some crumpled paper *(Show)* and next some small sticks *(Show)* and last some larger pieces of wood. *(Be arranging the fire as*

61

you are talking.) Now we could arrange our potatoes and corn around the fire. *(Do.)* But something was missing! What was it? "A match!" Brad said, "Bobetta, I need a match!" Oh yes, I had remembered the matches! And I gave him a whole box of matches. *(Matchbox without rough striking surface.)*

Boys and girls, these matches remind me of you and your mommy and daddy. Jesus has a bonfire all ready, and He has all kinds of people who need His love and His warmth. He has given us the job of lighting that fire. We are to be the little lights that will warm people up.

So I gave Brad the box of matches, and he put a match on the fire. *(Do.)* Is that what he did? No! How do you get the fire started? What do we have to do to the match? We have to scratch it to start the spark that will light it. *(Scratch match on smooth box surface.)* What's wrong? *(Scratch harder; then try the other side.)* What's wrong? *(Show that roughness has worn off the box.)* What has to be on the edge of this box to get the spark? That's right! A little rough place must be there. *(Let children feel the rough, then the smooth.)* Is it rough? No! About this time Brad said, "These matches are no good! I can't get a spark!"

Boys and girls, are we matches without a spark? Matches without a spark are no good. They can't get a fire started! What is it that gives us a spark? We have to be connected to Jesus. What is it that draws us close and connects us to Jesus? His Word! *(Hold up the Bible.)*

This little matchbox is smooth. It needs to be rough to get the spark. And boys and girls, Jesus can't give us that spark if we do it our own way—like when the box is smooth. The match has to be scratched on the rough surface. Sometimes the Bible seems rough to us. But that's the way to get the spark.

You know, I looked around in my purse and in all the nooks and crannies, and all I found were some more matches. But Brad didn't need the matches! All he needed was the connection!

Boys and girls, that's what we need today. We need that connection that will make the spark. It may be a little rough, but without it, we're no good as matches! Without that connection to Jesus, there will be no spark—no fire—and nobody will know Jesus' love and His warmth. This week, make sure you take time to get that connection to Jesus *(Hold up Bible)* so that you can be a match with a spark.

26
Bent Seed Pods

Scripture: Hebrews 12:1, 2.
Objects: Two long seed pods, one straight and one crooked; Bible.
Preparation: Keep the pods in a sack.
Introduction for Parents and Friends: Mommies, daddies, and friends, often there seem to be many ways to success, but if you will read Hebrews 12:1, 2 you will be assured that there is only one way.

Sermonette:

Boys and girls, what's the most important thing that your mommy and daddy must teach you while you're little like this? Do you know? It's the same most important thing that must be taught to older boys and girls. And you know, it's also the most important thing that mommies and daddies have to learn. What is it?

To learn about Jesus! We need to learn about Jesus so that we can love Him and trust Him with our lives. God has given us a couple of books to teach us about Him. What's the most well-known one? *(Hold up Bible.)* The Bible, that's right! But He's also given us another book. Does anybody know what that book is? That's right, *nature!*

I have something special from Jesus' book of nature. What is it? A seed pod! *(Show straight pod.)* Do you remember seeing these seed pods? How do they grow? *(Let*

65

child answer.) They hang down straight and long. Jesus has a plan for these seed pods. He wants them to grow down straight and long.

Eric, would you please hold this seed pod? *(Give child the straight one and let him hold it by the base.)* Where does the long, straight seed pod point? *(It will point up.)* To God! That's right! In the beginning, God planned for everything He made to point to Him. Not just the seed pod! His plan is for you and me to point to God too. He wants us to be tall and straight, and kind, loving, and truthful, so when others look at us they will see God.

But you know, there's somebody who wants to change God's way in everything. Who is it? Satan! That's right! Satan wants to change even seed pods so that they won't point to Jesus. Here is another seed pod. *(Pull out crooked seed pod and hold by base.)* Where is it pointing? To a person, not to God. Is it long and straight? No! It's not. It's bent and crooked. Why? Because it didn't follow Jesus' plan when it was growing. Remember, Jesus' plan is for it to grow down straight and long. But Satan got this little seed pod "hooked up" on something out there *(Show on pod)*, and so it grew out sideways. So now it is deformed and doesn't point nice and straight.

Boys and girls, Jesus has a plan for your life, just like the little seed pod. It's for you to be straight and long. Your mommies and daddies are training you to grow according to Jesus' plan. Obey them carefully so Satan won't "hook you up" and make you deformed like this little seed pod.

27
Dirty Face

Scripture: Revelation 21:6.
Objects: Dirt to smudge on face; pictures of mean faces and angry face; water and washcloths.
Preparation: Practice making your face dirty without a mirror. Have a mirror handy to check on cleanliness. Make sure that the container of water is large enough to not spill.
Introduction for Parents and Friends: Mommies, daddies, and friends, we often try to do the impossible. God never expects that of us. Please follow our lesson from Revelation 21:6.

Sermonette:

Have you ever gotten your face dirty? I mean real dirty, like this? *(Take wet mud and streak on your own face.)* Sure! We all have! Sometimes we know that we're going to get it dirty, and sometimes we don't mean to, but it gets dirty just the same. What's the first thing that your mommy wants to do when she sees your face looking like this? That's right, she wants to wash the dirt off. You know, boys and girls, Jesus wants us to have clean faces too. What do you think about this face? *(Show picture of mean boy's face.)* Does this boy have a clean face? No! He looks so mean! Here's a little girl. Does she have a clean face? *(Show picture of angry child.)* No! How can these children have kind, happy, clean faces? The same way that your mother gets your face clean when it's dirty. Does she just say, "Get that dirt off your face?" No! You can't get that dirt off by yourself any more than this boy can take his mean look off by himself. What does your mother use to take the dirt off? Water! *(Show container of water with wash cloth.)* That's right. She washes it very carefully. *(Take cloth and wash carefully.)*

Jesus says that He is the water of life. You can't wash your face without water, and these children can't have happy, kind faces without Jesus. Jesus is like the water to wash off the dirt. These children can't be kind and happy without Jesus. They must say, "Jesus, please take away my meanness and my anger." Like the water cleans your face, Jesus takes away their meanness. He leaves them with kind, happy faces.

Next time mother uses water to wash the dirt off of your face, remember that Jesus is like the water. You must have Jesus to wash the meanness and anger off of your face. You can't do it by yourself.

28
Peaches

Scriptures: Psalm 139:23, 24; 1 Chronicles 28:9.
Objects: Peaches; two small baskets; fruit crate with lid.
Preparation: Have two small baskets of peaches, one with all good fruit except for one that has a bad spot and the other basket with several rotten peaches. Have the baskets inside the wooden peach crate with the lid on it.
Introduction for Parents and Friends: While the children are coming up, parents and friends, there are two scriptures I'd like you to contemplate. The first is Psalm 139:23, 24. This is an account of David's personal involvement with God. Then in 1 Chronicles 28:9 we hear his advice, a man after God's own heart, to his offspring. This is the advice that we should live and exemplify to our children.

Sermonette:
Thursday I bought a whole crate of peaches at the market. Oh, they filled the whole car with a delicious smell. When I got home, I had many things to do, so I was happy when I opened the lid and saw that they were still quite green. That meant that I could leave them out a day or so and wouldn't have to put them in the refrigerator right away. But something disturbed me just a little. *(Take out a basket of peaches and pick through them.)* I noticed that one peach had a bad spot on it. *(Show peach*

69

with spot.) It wasn't a very big spot, and I was in such a hurry that I just put it back in and closed the lid. I went about my business. *(Put basket into crate and close the lid.)*

You know, boys and girls, this crate of peaches is like you and me! *(Slowly take out the first basket of peaches.)* We can look so pretty and smell so good, and many times nobody knows that there is some badness down inside of us. Nobody knows that there's some rottenness there. Maybe once in a while your temper flares up and you realize, "Oh! there's some badness in me." Or maybe you are very defiant and want your own way. It may not be a very big spot, but it's a spot in your character. *(Show spot on peach and replace peach and basket while talking.)*

Boys and girls, can the crate of peaches throw the rotten peach out? No! I have to take the spoiled peach out. It's just the same with you. You cannot take the bad trait out of your characters either. You must ask Jesus to take those rotten spots out of your characters. You must say, "Jesus, I was unkind to Jan; please take that little unkind spot out of me."

Do you know why we must ask Jesus to do that for us? Let's see what happens if we don't! Friday morning when I took the lid off the box, was I surprised! *(Remove lid and look in.)* That little spot was no longer little! It had gotten much bigger. *(Take out second basket of peaches.)* What was worse was that it had given a rotten spot to all the peaches around it! Now instead of one little rotten spot, look at all the rotten spots! *(Show all the rotten peaches.)*

Boys and girls, that's just the way it is in your lives. If you don't ask Jesus to take away that one little rotten spot, pretty soon your character is filled with lots of rotten spots. And that's why Jesus pleads with us to let Him take out the little rotten spots. Because, boys and girls, there are not going to be any rotten peaches in heaven, only sweet-smelling, beautiful, delicious ones. There are not going to be children with unkind, defiant, or temper-filled characters in heaven either. Jesus wants to take these spots out of your characters now.

Please don't close the lid on your characters with a spotted peach inside. *(**Replace basket and close lid.**)* Ask Jesus to take your spotted peaches out today.

29
Screws

Scripture: John 15:15.
Objects: Two screws; one magnet.
Preparation: Have the two screws in a little box with a lid. Keep the magnet in your hand.
Introduction for Parents and Friends: Mommies, daddies, and friends, have you ever found it difficult to be an effective comforter and friend? Ask God's Spirit to especially bless you as you meditate on John 15:15 this morning.

Sermonette:
This morning we're going to do some pretending. Do you like to pretend? Yes! We all like to pretend. Here are two little screws, and I'm going to pretend that they are people. *(Let child take out the screws.)* Let's stand them up. *(Stand them on the lid of the box.)* This one could be you, and this one your friend. You are standing up tall and straight. You are happy, you feel good, and you are glad that you are alive. But somehow Satan tempts your friend, and he gets sad and discouraged and feels down and out. *(Lay one of the screws down on its side.)* Have you ever felt like that before? Have you ever wished that somebody would cheer you up, give you something to live for, give you some hope? Well, you know, Jesus says that that's what friends are for, to encourage each other, to pick each other up, to cheer each other. So

Jesus has asked us to be friends; He wants us to do this. But He's also warned us, "Don't try doing it by yourself. When a person is down and feeling blue, don't try picking him up by yourself. You may get discouraged, too, if you do."

Let's see if you can pick your friend up on your own. Shall we try? *(Try picking up one screw using the other.)* It's impossible. And the harder you try, the more frustrated you become, until you almost say, "Jesus doesn't know what He's talking about! I can't be a friend and cheer someone up. I try so hard and it doesn't seem to help!" But you've forgotten what Jesus said. He says that you can't really help someone who needs help without His help. "You have to have Me!" He says.

Now, let's try it again. Here you are, and early in the morning, before you go to your friend's house, you make time for Jesus. We'll pretend that this little magnet is Jesus. You talk to Jesus and say, "Jesus, come and be with me today." What happens? Jesus is with you! Whenever we ask Jesus to be with us, He is there immediately! *(Place screw in contact with magnet.)* So now, Jesus is with you; you aren't doing things by yourself. You go to your friend's house and see him so down and discouraged. Since you and Jesus are connected, what happens? *(Lift screw lying down by touching it with end of first screw connected to magnet.)* Yes! Now you can lift up your friend! You can say the right words of encouragement.

When you're not connected to Jesus *(Remove magnet from first screw)* it's impossible to lift up a person that is down. Jesus wants you to be a friend to discouraged people, and He reminds you, "Without Me you can't do it!" So boys and girls, get connected with Jesus first! *(Put first screw next to magnet.)* Make time to talk to Him and ask Him to be with you. The first thing every morning, before you go out and try to be a friend, connect with Jesus, and you'll have the strength and power to be a *real* friend. *(Lift second screw with first one.)*

30
A New Creature

Scripture: 2 Corinthians 5:17.
Objects: Caterpillar; full chrysalis, empty chrysalis, butterfly.
Preparation: Have a live caterpillar on a cabbage leaf in a jar.
Introduction for Parents and Friends: Mothers, fathers, and friends, our lesson is found in 2 Corinthians 5:17 this morning. Perhaps you can think on why something so easy and natural for caterpillars seems so difficult for human beings.

Sermonette:
Boys and girls, Jesus has a life plan for every little bird, animal, and insect. He has a life plan for you and me. His plan is that we do what He wants us to do, not what we want to do.

Do you know what I found on a cabbage leaf in my garden? *(Show caterpillar.)* That's right! A caterpillar. Caterpillars usually aren't very pretty. What is the caterpillar doing? That's right! He's eating. I like to eat, and you like to eat. Some people, however, want to be slim and trim, and yet want to eat whatever they please and whenever they please. Like this caterpillar, eating seems the most important thing in life. But Jesus has a different plan for people, just as He has a different plan for caterpillars. Caterpillars obey Jesus' plan. It is natural for them to do so, but you don't have to. You can choose not to follow Jesus' plan.

Jesus tells this little caterpillar, and He tells us, "If you do what I want you to do, and, not what you want to do, I'll make you into a beautiful creature. I can change you from what you are into something beautiful."

This little caterpillar says, "Jesus, how can that be possible? I can't fly!" And Jesus says, "You're right, *you* can't fly! But you let me be in charge of your life, and I can do the impossible. *I'll* make you fly, and when you do, you'll be a whole new creature! You won't be a caterpillar anymore."

So the little caterpillar thinks, "I love eating cabbage leaves! Do I really want Jesus to change me?"

But boys and girls, caterpillars *always* let Jesus change them. Do you know what they do? They stop trying to do everything themselves. They lie very still and let Jesus work, and He begins changing them. While Jesus is changing them, what do they look like? *(Show full chrysalis.)* Is the caterpillar inside the chrysalis running around doing things his own way? Is he eating and trying to look pretty? No! He looks as if he were dead.

Boys and girls, Jesus says that we must let Him change us, like He changed the caterpillar into a dead-looking cocoon. But do you know what's going to happen to this chrysalis that looks dead? Pretty soon a new creature will come out of it. Here's an empty chrysalis. *(Show empty chrysalis.)* Now look at what comes out of the dead-looking chrysalis. *(Show butterfly.)* A beautiful butterfly! Does it crawl around on the ground like a caterpillar? No, it flies gracefully through the air. It doesn't stuff itself on cabbage leaves anymore. It has been changed and now looks beautiful.

Next time you children see a caterpillar, remember that the caterpillar always follows Jesus' plan, and Jesus changes him into a beautiful butterfly or moth. Why don't you decide to follow Jesus' plan and let Him make you into a beautiful creature too?

31
Dirty Clothes

Scripture: Jeremiah 2:13.
Objects: Dirty blouse; jar of water; picture of a woman in an extravagant party dress.
Preparation: Make sure that the blouse is very dirty. Have the water in a jar.
Introduction for Parents and Friends: Parents and friends, you may follow along with our lesson by reading Jeremiah 2:13.

Sermonette:
My, you all look so lovely today! You have your special Sabbath clothes on. What would you think if I came to church with this blouse on? *(Put dirty blouse on over clothes.)* Is this something that I should wear? No! Why? That's right. It's dirty. All that you see when you look at me is the blouse. Boys and girls, do you know that Jesus is interested in what I wear? He's interested in what you wear. He doesn't want us to wear things that call attention to ourselves. When you look at this picture, what is the first thing you see? *(Show picture of woman in an extravagant party dress.)* That's right, the dress! Shoddy clothes as well as extravagant clothes draw attention to ourselves.

What has to be done to my blouse so that I can wear it and you wouldn't stare at it? That's right! I'll have to use water to wash it. *(Hold up jar of water.)* You know,

Jesus tells us that He is like water. If we ask Him to, He will clean up our clothes, so that what we wear will be decent and appropriate. We can't change our habits of dress by ourselves any more than this blouse can clean itself. But just as the water cleans up the blouse, so Jesus can change our way of dressing to be neat and appropriate, to call attention to our characters and not to our clothes.

32
Pica Pica

Scripture: Proverbs 8:33.
Objects: Pica pica vine; pica pica pods.
Preparation: Keep the pica pica pods in plastic bag so that they can be seen but not cause irritation. Arrange for someone to warn against touching the pods.
Introduction to Parents and Friends: Mothers, fathers, and friends, respecting authority and instruction can be difficult for some people, but perhaps today's lesson from Proverbs 8:33 will help you.

Sermonette:
Boys and girls, have you ever wanted to do something that seemed so much fun, that looked so interesting, but your mommy or daddy said, "No! That's dangerous; you mustn't do that"? Has that ever happened to you? *(Acknowledge responses.)* Maybe it was jumping up and down on your bed or riding your Big Wheel out in the road or crossing the street by yourself. I don't know—there are many thing that mommies and daddies say No! to, and sometimes we don't like to hear them tell us not to. We want to do what we want to do anyway. We can't see anything wrong with it.

Well, boys and girls, Jesus tells us that it is wise to listen to instructions from our mommies and daddies. Jesus has given us something to remind us next time we don't want to listen to instruction. *(Show vine.)* There is a beautiful vine that grows around our house. It has such pretty flowers. After the flowers disappear, seed pods come on. And the seed pods soon turn brown and develop what looks like the softest fur on them. They look so soft and fuzzy—you might think it would be nice to rub the pod across your face. Here are a couple of pods. *(Take plastic out of bag concealing it.)* Would you like me to give you one? *(Act as if you were going to open the plastic bag and take them out. Have somebody yell, "No! that's pica pica! Don't touch it!")* Why can't I touch it? It looks so pretty and furry! *(Have a child say, "But it itches and itches. Don't touch it!")* Eric has given me some instruction. He told me not to touch that little furry pod, that it will make me itch! Jesus tells me in the Bible to listen to *Eric's* instruction and be wise. But what if I decide that *Eric* doesn't know what he's talking about? What if I go on ahead and feel this little furry pod? What's going to happen? *(Let children comment.)* Yes! I'll itch terribly! Once I try it, I'll never touch pica pica again, that's for sure!

Boys and girls, Jesus wants to keep us from the terrible problems that can happen to us. He's given us the pica pica pods to remind us that, even if something looks so pretty and inviting, it may not be good for us. He has given us mommies and daddies to warn us to stay away from things that will hurt us. He wants us to listen to their instructions so that we won't get into terrible problems. *(Scratch yourself all over as if affected by the pica pica.)*

During this next week, I want you to "hear instruction and be wise." OK?

33
Water, a Necessity

Scripture: John 4:10.
Objects: Several dirty dishes; pitcher of water; picture of plate of food.
Preparation: Have the dirty dishes in a bag on a tray with the water.
Introduction for Parents and Friends: Parents and friends, you may follow today's lesson in John 4:10.

Sermonette:
Boys and girls, Jesus has told us that we must have Him in our lives. He gives us things to remind us of how important He is. What is this? *(Show pitcher with water.)* That's right! It's water. Jesus tells us that He is the living Water, but some people think that they don't need Him. What is this? *(Show dirty plate.)* What a dirty plate! How many of you help your mothers wash the dishes? Good! Then you know that the plate can't clean itself. How can the plate be made clean? That's right, by washing it in water. You have to put water on it to clean it. Jesus says that He is the water. He will make our plates clean.

(Picture of plate of food with meat, wine, etc.) Do you know what this is? A plate of food. Some people think they know what to put on their plates to eat. They think they can eat the proper things without Jesus. But unless we let Jesus help us, we may eat all kinds of "yucky"

81

things that are not good for us without knowing it—things that He doesn't want us to eat. When people learn about the things that they shouldn't eat, some of them find it hard to quit eating them.

We can't take these no-good things off our plates unless Jesus helps us. He is the living Water that will clean up our plates so that we will eat the way that we should.

Next time you go to help your mother wash the dishes, remember that the water is like Jesus. And that just as water cleans the dishes, Jesus wants to clean our plates so that we will eat only the things that are most healthful and clean for us.

34
Satan

Scripture: Psalm 91:14, 15.
Objects: Picture of Satan; picture of large black mamba snake; an orange.
Preparation: None.
Introduction for Parents and Friends: Mothers, fathers, and friends, Jesus has never promised us that we would not have troubles, but today's lesson, found in Psalm 91:14, 15, explains His solution to our problems.

Sermonette:

Who do you think this picture represents? *(Show picture of Satan.)* Satan! That's right. Does he look kind and thoughtful? No! He looks mean to me. Does Satan love you? No! Does Satan want you to live forever? No! What does Satan want to do to you? He would like to destroy you. The Bible describes Satan as a creature that likes to kill, a deadly creature. Can anybody think of what that creature could be? I have a picture of it! A snake! That's right. *(Show picture of black mamba.)* The Bible calls Satan a serpent, a snake. He is like the black mamba snake of Africa. This black mamba is a big snake. It grows to be as much as twelve feet long. It is also one of the most poisonous snakes in the world. What does "poisonous" mean? *(Wait for responses.)* That's right, if it bites you, you die. Isn't Satan like that? He wants you to die. The mamba is a fast snake. Some people say that it can travel as fast as 20 mph. It doesn't just sit back and wait; it attacks anything that comes into its territory. Isn't that just the way Satan does? Yes.

Who is it that wants us to live, to live forever? Jesus. Jesus has promised us that if we will trust Him, He will help keep Satan's bites from killing us. As long as we live on this earth, we are living in Satan's territory. Satan will do all he can to bite us. But Jesus has promised that He'll keep those deadly bites of Satan from killing us.

It's sort of like the man in Africa who left his house one morning. But before he left, he put a big orange in his pocket. *(Show orange.)* As he was walking along, a big black mamba attacked swiftly, injected its poison, and quickly disappeared. The man stood there shocked, watching the snake disappear and realizing that in five minutes he would be dead. But, since he didn't feel anything he looked down and suddenly realized that the snake had bitten the orange *(Show orange)* and injected all its poison into the orange. Oh, how happy and thankful that man was! He didn't have to die.

Boys and girls, that's the way we should feel this morning—happy and thankful because Jesus keeps Satan's bites from killing us. He has promised us that if we ask Him to be with us every morning and take Him with us, when Satan strikes like a deadly mamba, Jesus will be like the orange and keep his bite from killing us.

35
Spider Webs

Scriptures: Job 8:13, 14; Psalm 118:8.
Objects: Pictures of spiders in web; picture of spider spinnerets; picture of web.
Preparation: Have the pictures well marked and show them slowly enough so that all the children can see.
Introduction for Parents and Friends: Mommies, daddies, and friends, our lesson today is found in Job 8:13, 14 and Psalm 118:8. We'd like you to ask yourselves on whose strength you're depending.

Sermonette:

Some of Jesus' creatures are very small, but we can learn from them. The spider is a wise and talented creature. *(Show pictures of spiders.)* Jesus has given him six or eight spinnerets under his abdomen *(Show picture of spinnerets)* to spin a silky thread. *(Show picture of web.)* For its thickness, spider silk is one of the strongest materials known. How many of you have seen a spider hanging on its own silk? *(Show picture of spider in web.)* It seems to keep the spider from falling.

How many of you have seen a lovely, symmetrical spider web? *(Show picture of web.)* It looks very beautiful and special. But Jesus has warned us of something. He tells us that you and I may be like the spider. This spider is trusting its web to keep it from falling. You know, some people trust in themselves to keep from falling into sin.

They try really hard to be good, and many times, like the spider, their silk threads seem to hold them up. But what happens if somebody big comes along and goes like this to the spider's silk? *(Move hand as if breaking web.)* The spider falls. And who's more powerful, we or Satan? Satan is, and when he comes along and goes like this *(Move hand)* to us and we're trying to be good all by ourselves, what happens to us? We fall! Just like the spider. The only way for us to be able to stay happy, kind, and obedient when Satan attacks us is to trust in Jesus to make our web and to be our silk. Who is bigger and stronger, Satan or Jesus? Jesus is! And if you are asking Jesus to be your happiness, kindness, and obedience, when Satan comes along, he won't be able to break the silk that Jesus makes because Jesus is more powerful than Satan.

Next time you see a spider or its web, I want you to think, "Is my goodness like the spider's web? Am I doing it myself? Or am I trusting in Jesus and His goodness?"

36
Idols

Scripture: 1 Samuel 15:22, 23.
Objects: Picture of witch and Saul; picture of idol worshipers; idol.
Preparation: In a basket have an image that looks like an idol.
Introduction for Parents and Friends: Parents and friends, we'd like you to follow our theme by reading 1 Samuel 15:22, 23. Perhaps you have never realized the seriousness of stubbornness and rebellion in God's eyes.

Sermonette:
(Let child take idol out of basket.) What is this? An idol. What is an idol? *(Let children answer.)* People worship it as God. Here is a picture of people worshiping idols. *(Show picture.)* I don't worship idols. Do you? No! I wouldn't think of it! But I want to ask you something. Have you ever been mad at your mommy? Have you ever thought, "I'm not going to do what she wants me to do! I'm going to do what *I* want to do!"? When you feel like that, we call that being stubborn or being rebellious. But do you know what Jesus calls that? He calls being stubborn like worshiping idols and being rebellious like visiting a witch. Do you remember the story of a king who visited a witch? *(Show picture of Saul and witch.)* That's right, King Saul! In this picture was King Saul a special friend of Jesus? No! Do you know why? He started out by being

stubborn and rebellious. He did what he wanted to do and not what Jesus had asked him to do. And he ended up visiting a witch.

Boys and girls, your mommies and daddies stand in the place of God to you. When they ask you to do something and you are stubborn and rebellious, it's like being stubborn and rebellious toward God. God tells us that being stubborn is just as bad as worshiping idols. I don't want to worship idols, and I know that you don't want to either. So remember next time that you feel like doing what you want to and not what mommy and daddy want you to do, Jesus says that feeling like that is just like worshiping idols or visiting a witch.

I don't want you to be idol worshipers, so let's choose to obey and do as Mommy and Daddy ask us rather than being rebellious and stubborn idol worshipers.

37
Cemeteries

Scripture: Luke 11:44.
Objects: Pictures of Jesus with children, green lawn, cemetery; several dry bones.
Preparation: Have the bones in a small sack.
Introduction for Parents and Friends: Parents and friends, we'd like you to enjoy our story too. You may follow our lesson from the Bible in Luke 11:44.

Sermonette:
Boys and girls, do you ever suppose that Jesus called anybody names? I mean bad names. We know that Jesus was the most thoughtful person there ever was. He was the most gentle, loving, and kind person that ever lived. Remember, the children liked to be with Him. *(Show picture.)* Do children like to be with mean people? No! But the Bible tells us of a time when Jesus went to a Pharisee's house to eat dinner. There were other Pharisees and scribes there too, and Jesus was talking to them. The longer He talked, the more frustrated and upset He got inside. I can just see Him talking to them nicely, but they weren't listening. I can imagine that He finally raised His finger and looked them right in the eye. *(Shake finger.)* He called them a name. He called them hypocrites, and then He went on to say, "You're just like this!" *(Show picture of green lawn.)* What is this? A lovely green lawn. No, it's not! You think it's a beautiful

green lawn, and everybody thought that the Pharisees were God's beautiful people, but Jesus was warning them that, although they looked like a beautiful lawn on the outside, what were they underneath? They were really this! *(Show picture of cemetery.)* What's this? A cemetery! A cemetery is full of what? Graves. And what's inside a grave? *(Show several bones.)* Bones! Are bones alive? No! Bones are dead. Jesus called those Pharisees graves. He said, "Outside you look like a beautiful green lawn, and people can't even tell, but inside you are a grave. There's nothing but dead bones inside you. You're dead! I want you to be alive inside!"

Boys and girls, Jesus wants you to be alive inside! If Jesus were here today, would He call you a grave? Those Pharisees went to church every Sabbath; they paid their tithes and offerings; they learned their memory verses— but they were dead inside. Do you know why? Where do we get life from? Who is life? Jesus is life! And boys and girls, those Pharisees didn't love Jesus. They didn't ask Him to come into their hearts. They didn't let Jesus change them.

Do you have Jesus in your heart? Do you talk to Jesus every day? Do you study Jesus' Word? Or are you full of bones? *(Show bones.)* Are you dead inside?

I can't tell by looking on the outside. You all look like lovely green lawns to me. But this next week, make time for Jesus to come inside you so you won't be like a grave with dead bones. OK?

38
You Are Important

Scripture: Psalm 139:14.
Objects: Many little seashells; blackboard; chalk.
Preparation: These shells need not be perfect. The children are delighted just to get something. Be sure to let several of them respond.
Introduction for Parents and Friends: Parents and friends, we'd like for you to follow our lesson. You may turn to Psalm 139:14.

Sermonette:

Are you sometimes sad? Do you sometimes feel like nobody loves you, like nobody cares what happens to you?

This morning I have something Jesus made to give to each one of you. I want you to keep it in a special place; and every time you start feeling sad, lonely, or like nobody loves you or cares, I want you to get it out.

Now hold out your hand and close it immediately—we won't look until everybody has gotten one. *(Give each child a tiny shell.)*

Now open your hand and let's all look. What do you have in your hand? A shell! Is it a big shell? No! It is a very little shell! In fact, it's so little that you can easily hide it in your hand.

Now open your hand again and let's look at our little shell. Let's look at the shape first. Is it a plain old square shape? *(Draw a square on board.)* No! Is it a plain circle? *(Draw a circle.)* No! Not even a circle. How about a rectangle? *(Draw a rectangle.)* No! It's hard to describe the shape of your shell. It has such a special shape. In fact, if you look at your friend's little shell, it's probably not even the same shape as yours!

Jesus made your little shell with a special shape all its own because He loves it. Don't you think He loves you as much as He loves this little shell?

Let's look at our little shell again. What color is it? Is it just plain old black? No! Is it just plain old white? No. Maybe it's just brown? No. Let's see how many colors Jesus put into our little shells. He loved each little, tiny shell enough to give it many pretty colors. *(Let children report on colors they see.)*

Your little shell is special. Don't you think that you're even more special to Jesus than your little, tiny shell? But, you know, some people forget to remind themselves how very special *they* are to Jesus. Keep your little shell so that it may remind you just how special you are to Jesus.

39
Eclipses

Scripture: 2 Corinthians 4:3, 4.
Objects: Large spotlight; globe of world; picture of full moon.
Preparation: None.
Introduction for Parents and Friends: It's amazing how the natural world reveals the things of God to us! Please follow our lesson today in 2 Corinthians 4:3, 4.

Sermonette:

How many of you saw the moon last night? A full moon is so pretty. *(Show picture.)* Let's let *Tim* represent the moon. *(Child should stand.)* Did you know that the moon has no light of its own? And that's like *Timmy* too. Is *Timmy* shining? No! Where does the moon get its light from? It gets its light from the sun.

So, where do we get our light from? From the Son of God, Jesus. *(Turn spotlight onto child's face.)* See how *Timmy's* face shines! Now, what happens if something, like our world, comes between the sun and the moon? *(Put globe between child and spotlight.)* The sun doesn't shine on the moon now. And the same thing happens if we let the things of the world come between us and God's Son, Jesus. Our faces won't shine. What happens if *Timmy* looks away from Jesus? His face gets dark.

Boys and girls, we must keep looking directly at Jesus, the Light, not to anybody else, or our faces will not shine with happiness and beauty.

Next time you look at the moon, remember that it is only as you look directly at the true Light, that you too can shine.

40
Squash Seed

Scriptures: Mark 4:30-32; Romans 14:17.
Objects: Squash seeds.
Preparation: None.
Introduction for Parents and Friends: Mothers, fathers, and friends, there is a lesson about good seed giving good fruit in Mark 4:30-32 and Romans 14:17, our texts for today.

Sermonette:
How many of you want to be good boys and girls? Let me see your hands. *(Acknowledge hands.)* Everyone wants to be good! But sometimes that seems so hard. You think, "I'm going to only speak kind words today." Then Mommy asks you to dump the trash and, oh how you fuss and whine, because you don't want to do it. Or maybe someone makes fun of you and teases you. Instead of turning away, you get angry and hit him.

Did you know that Jesus has good news for boys and girls, mommies and daddies who try so hard to be good, but just can't seem to do the right thing?

What do I have here? *(Show squash seed.)* A squash seed. It's small. It doesn't seem like anything good could come from something so small. But what happens if you put this tiny seed in the ground? Pretty soon some tiny green leaves come up, and then more and more and more! And that vine gets bigger and bigger. And pretty flowers come, and then some squash. In fact, if you let this squash vine grow, pretty soon the only thing you would see in your yard would be a squash vine!

Now, what is Jesus' promise for you? He says that if you ask Him, He will come right into your heart, and it will be just like putting a tiny seed in the ground. As you let Jesus be in your life each day, His love will grow and grow and grow inside you. Your life will be beautiful, like the pretty green vine, and it will produce good works, just like the squash vine grew squash. And none of this happened because you tried so hard, but because Jesus' love was growing inside you.

Instead of hitting little sister, you will be patient. Instead of whining when Daddy asks you to do something, you will cheerfully obey.

Now, let me ask one more question. Out where my squash grows are some weeds. Suppose that one day one of these weeds looked at the squash vine and thought, "I like that pretty green leaf and the big fruit. I'm going to make a squash like that." Could the weed do that? No, of course not! To make a squash you must be a squash plant.

That's Jesus' good news for us. If we want to be good, we will never be good by acting like the weed and thinking we can make a beautiful squash plant in our own strength. Rather, we will ask Jesus to plant His tiny love seed inside us, and we will ask Him to keep it growing there every day. Then we will do the right things.

41
The Penguin's Swimming Pool

Scripture: 1 Corinthians 10:13.
Objects: Pan of water with large piece of ice; picture of penguins.
Preparation: None.
Introduction for Parents and Friends: Parents, friends, have you ever found yourself in a situation for which you saw no way of escape? Let's look at 1 Corinthians 10:13 to see what Jesus does for us in such situations.

Sermonette:
What do you see in this pan of water? *(Show pan with ice.)* Yes a big piece of ice! Who wants to feel this water? *(Let children feel water.)* It's cold. Who would like to take a bath in this water? It's much too cold.

But did you know there is a bird that swims where there is ice in the water? He lives down in the Antarctic, where the ocean is filled with gigantic ice chunks called icebergs. Can anyone tell me its name? *(Show picture.)* Yes, it is the penguin.

Now if I were that penguin standing on the edge of the ice looking into that water filled with ice, I'm afraid I would think: "Oh, it's too cold. I can't go swimming today." However, Mr. Penguin knows that he must go swimming, for in that water is his food. And Mr. Penguin

97

also knows something else—something that you and I sometimes forget. He knows that whatever God expects of him, God will make possible.

You see, God has given Mr. Penguin a thick layer of feathers and fat to keep him warm while he is swimming in his icy bath. God has provided a way for Mr. Penguin to live, even in this most difficult land of ice and snow and freezing water.

You know, in the same way God gives Mr. Penguin what he needs to swim in icy water, He will give you what you need, even in situations that seem impossible. Maybe your best friend asks you to do something sneaky and wrong. What can you do? You can ask God for strength to say No, and He will give you strength to say No, even though your friend laughs at you and maybe won't be your friend anymore. Like Mr. Penguin's feathers, God will make a way for you to get through that experience which seems to you like icy water.

There are many other difficult experiences I can think of that you children, and even your mommies and daddies, will meet, for loving Jesus does not mean that everything will always be happy and easy. But, when these troubles come, I want you to think of Mr. Penguin and God's concern and care for him. Then remember that God loves you too and will also take care of you and give you what you need to get through the icy times of your life.

42
The Bicycle Instruction Book

Scripture: Psalm 119:105.
Objects: Bicycle handlebar; rubber hand grip; hot water; Bible; instruction book for bicycle assembly.
Preparation: Ask a man and a woman to help with the rubber hand grip. Bring hot water in a thermos.
Introduction for Parents and Friends: Mothers, fathers, and friends, God has given us His Word to guide us through life. Our lesson today is found in Psalm 119:105.

Sermonette:

How many of you sometimes wonder how things were made, what will happen in the future, how to act if you see something you want very much but don't have money to buy it, or how to behave if daddy asks you to do something you don't want to do? All of these are big questions about living life in God's way. I have many questions for which I would like answers, and I imagine you do too. How can we know the answers?

Who knows what this is? *(**Hold up handlebar.**)* Yes, of course, it's a bicycle handlebar. I once heard about a boy who received a new bicycle for Christmas, but it was all apart in a big box. Now, if you received a new bicycle for Christmas, you would want to ride it—wouldn't you? But it would have to be put together, and that might be hard for you to do.

The boy who received the bike for Christmas found one thing that looked easy to do. He knew that the rubber hand grip fits on the end of the handlebar. So he grabbed it and pushed *(Have child try to push rubber handgrip onto the bar)*—and pushed—and pushed. But it wouldn't go on—at least not far enough to stay on. So Mommy tried. *(Woman tries to put it on.)* Then Daddy was called to try. *(Man tries to put it on.)* But still it wouldn't go on! It would go on a little bit, but not much. What a problem! It seemed like a very simple thing to do, but it wouldn't go on.

Now how should we solve this problem—this question? Does anyone know? Yes, we need to read the book of instructions. *(Show instruction book.)* We have ignored it while we've been trying to put on the hand grip our way. But now we've decided to read the instructions. *(Open instruction book.)* "Run hot water over the rubber hand grip; then slide onto the handlebar." Oh-h-h! This is the answer to our problem! We've been doing it our way, and it hasn't worked! Do you think it will work if we follow the directions? *(Acknowledge affirmative answers.)*

(Open thermos of hot water.) I have some hot water in here. *(Show children and then immerse handle grip for 30-45 seconds. Then have child push onto handlebar.)* The instruction book had the answer for us all the time.

Let's think again about the questions we have about life. Who do you think has the answers? God! Jesus! Yes. And has God given us an instruction book? *(Hold up Bible.)* Yes, the Bible. But the Bible can't answer your questions or help solve your problems if you don't read it.

This week make sure to read the instruction book God has given you.

43
Patterns

Scripture: 1 Peter 2:21.
Objects: Pattern; yardage; scissors.
Preparation: Have a dress pattern and yardage that you can cut up.
Introduction for Parents and Friends: Parents and friends, please follow along with our lesson from 1 Peter 2:21 and see how it can help you with your New Year's resolutions.

Sermonette:
Who knows what this is *(Hold up a pattern.)* It's a pattern. Have you ever seen your mommy use a pattern before? What does she use it for? Right, to make a dress, a shirt. This is a pattern that I used to make a dress. First I laid the pattern on the material *(Do it)* and pinned it carefully *(Do it)* and then cut it out, being careful to follow the lines. *(Cut one piece out.)* And then I followed the directions, doing just as they told me to do. When I got through, I had a pretty dress.

What did I have when I finished? Did I have a pair of pants? a bathing suit? No! Why? Because I used a dress pattern, I had a dress when I finished.

Boys and girls, Jesus wants you and me to be happy, and He knows that we will be happiest if we are like Him. He is our pattern, and what is the instruction book? The Bible. We won't be happy if we try to be like the boy or girl who doesn't know Jesus and doesn't read the Bible. Do you know why?

Well, what if I were to say, "I'm going to make a dress, but I don't need this pattern and I don't need the instruction book either. I'll just do it my own way." How do you think the dress would come out? Here I start cutting *(Cut at random.)* And, oh, what a mess. It's too much work to sew! I'll just make the dress without sewing it. It's much easier that way. *(Keep cutting.)* Maybe, I think I have a real pretty dress, but let's hold it up and look at it. *(Hold up cut-up yardage.)* Ugh! Is this a pretty dress? No!

Boys and girls, in our living we have to have a pattern too! If we try to live without following a pattern, we'll look like this—just awful!

Who is going to be your pattern? Jesus! That's right. And what is your instruction book?—the Bible. And when you follow Jesus and the Bible, your lives won't be the terrible mess that this is!

44
Thanksgiving, I

Scripture: Hebrews 13:15.
Objects: Picture of altar with lamb; picture of Pilgrims; cardboard with circle cut out.
Preparation: Have the cardboard large enough to hide a person's face and upper torso. The circle is just big enough to show the lips.
Introduction for Parents and Friends: Mommies, daddies, and friends, did you think that the sacrificial system was done away with? Please follow our lesson from Hebrews 13:15.

Sermonette:
Can anybody remember what was special about this week? That's right! Last Thursday was Thanksgiving Day. Some people think that the Pilgrims celebrated the first Thanksgiving when they gave thanks to God for preserving them through a cold, hard winter. *(Show picture of Pilgrims.)* But long before the Pilgrims came to America in 1620, God had told the children of Israel to set aside a whole week for giving thanks. Part of the thanksgiving ceremony was to offer sacrifices.

When you think of sacrifices, you think of an altar. *(Show picture of altar.)* And you think of a lamb. The children of Israel sacrificed animals, because that's what God asked them to do. But did you know that God asks you and me to offer sacrifices too? What do we use for a sacrifice? Shall I show you? *(Call up a child and hold cardboard in front of face with just lips showing through the hole.)* Nowadays Jesus asks us to sacrifice our lips, our mouths, our bodies, instead of animals.

How do you suppose that you could give a sacrifice with your mouth? By saying thankful words, happy words and words of praise!

Do we have any little lips here this morning that want to be a sacrifice? Can anybody say some thankful words for me? *(Let several children talk through the cardboard circle.)*

Let's remember, it's nice to be thankful on Thanksgiving Day, but Jesus wants to hear our sacrifices of thanksgiving every day!

45
Thanksgiving, II

Scripture: Matthew 25:40.
Objects: Picture of Pilgrims; fresh fruits and vegetables; picture of altar; large basket; large heart cut out of red cardboard.
Preparation: Have a large sack filled with fresh fruit and vegetables. Have a basket the right size to make a beautiful arrangement and leave it up all during the service.
Introduction for Parents and Friends: Parents and friends, our thankfulness to God can be shown in many ways. Please enjoy our lesson with us by reading Matthew 25:40.

Sermonette:
This is a special weekend, isn't it? Why? That's right! It's Thanksgiving weekend. Did you have a big special dinner on Thanksgiving? Why do we celebrate Thanksgiving? *(Let children respond.)* We're remembering how God took care of the Pilgrims who came to the New World. In the fall, after God had blessed them with a bountiful harvest, they showed God how thankful they were by sharing their food with the Indians in a big dinner. Let's see what gifts the Pilgrims brought to thank God for taking care of them. *(Have children put fruits and vegetables into basket.)* They showed how thankful they were by giving God some of the vegetables. How

did they give their vegetables to God? Did they put them on top of an altar and burn them up? That's what the children of Israel did. They had thanksgiving offerings, and they put their offerings onto an altar. *(Show picture of altar.)* But how did the Pilgrims show their thankfulness to God? They shared their food with the Indians in a giant feast. When we share what we have with others, we are sharing with God.

What Thanksgiving offering did you bring to Jesus this morning? Did you bring some vegetables to share with your friends? What kind of a Thanksgiving offering *can* you give? What does Jesus want from boys and girls? Jesus wants your heart. *(Show large heart.)* How do you give your heart to Him? Well, first you tell Him that you want to give it to Him. Shall we do that right now? *(Pray a short prayer.)* Now what do we do? We do what the Pilgrims did. We share with others. They shared their food that Jesus had given them. We'll share the happiness, the kindness, the thoughtfulness, the courtesy that Jesus gives us when we give Him our hearts. We'll share with others.

When you go home from church today, remember that part of your Thanksgiving offering is sharing Jesus' love with mommy, daddy, and your friends.

46
Christmas Lights

Scripture: Matthew 5:14.

Objects: Several Christmas tree balls; several Christmas ornaments.

Preparation: Have the Sabbath School Christmas tree up in the front of the church with its lights on. Small white lights are best.

Introduction for Parents and Friends: Mommies, daddies, and friends, Christmas is a perfect time for object lessons. As you read Matthew 5:14 and think about our lesson today, perhaps you can think of other familiar objects to relate thoughts of Jesus to.

Sermonette:

We're having our story over here by the Christmas tree today. How many of you have Christmas trees in your house? *(Acknowledge hands.)* Is your tree just a plain, green tree? No! What do you have on your tree, *Timmy?* Christmas balls! What color are the balls on your tree, *Eric? (Await response.)* Our Christmas tree has pretty Christmas balls on it too. *(Hang some balls on the tree.)*

What else does your tree have on it? *(Let children answer.)* Ornaments! *(Show.)* These make the tree pretty. *(Hang several on tree.)* But what is the prettiest thing about Christmas and Christmas trees? The lights! Right! *(Turn out the lights on tree.)* This tree isn't nearly as pretty without lights. What do the lights on the Christmas tree remind you of? They remind us of what we should be. *You* are like the lights on the Christmas tree. Jesus says, "You are the light of the world." *(Turn on the lights.)* Isn't the tree much prettier when the lights are on? Without the lights *(Turn off the lights)* this Christmas tree isn't very pretty.

But Jesus' special boys and girls are like lights on the Christmas tree. *(Turn on the lights.)* By having happy faces, speaking kind words, and doing helpful deeds they make any place beautiful.

This Christmas season, when you see all the pretty lights, remember that Jesus wants your happy faces and cheerful words to be the lights for His Christmas tree.

47
Christmas Gifts *

Scripture: John 3:16.
Objects: Three wrapped presents.
Preparation: The first present is a boy's shirt; the second present is a box with oranges, apples, and bananas; and the third present is a picture of Jesus with a child.
Introduction for Parents and Friends: Mothers, fathers, and friends, Christmas is for giving. Did you think about God's gift to you this Christmas? Today's lesson is found in John 3:16.

Sermonette:

How many of you like Christmas? Did you have a fun Christmas? Did you get lots of presents? Did you give away some presents too? It's fun to give and get presents. Did you know that one Christmas day God gave you a special present? Did your Mommy and Daddy remind you of that present? God gave you a super-special present, a perfect present.

I have three presents up here. Let's see if any of these is the special present that God gave you on Christmas day. *(Have a child open the first present.)* This surely is a pretty package. Do you suppose God's present was in a pretty package? We're told that it was wrapped in a perfect package. *(Have child show shirt.)*

Oh, what a pretty shirt! Do you suppose that God gave

---

* For use on the first Sabbath after Christmas.

you a shirt for Christmas? No! Why not? Would Shelly want to wear this shirt? No! It's a boy's shirt, and God's gift was for both boys and girls. And this shirt fits Eric fine, but can Timmy wear it? No! It's too small. God's gift isn't a shirt. His gift is perfect whether you are big like Timmy or small like Eric. No! God's gift couldn't be clothes.

(Have child open second package.) Joey is having to work a little to open this present. You know, God's present is like that. It takes a little effort to get inside and find the present. What's inside your package, Joey? Oh! Some lovely fruit—apples, oranges, and bananas. Is this God's special Christmas gift to you? Oh, God gave it to you, but is it His special Christmas gift? No! Why not? What happens if Joey eats up the apple? Will he still have God's special gift? No! It will be all gone, and we're told that we will always have God's special gift. It will never be all gone. And what will happen to Joey's banana if he doesn't eat it pretty soon? It will rot. Will God's special gift ever be "yucky" to us? No! It's always sweet and precious.

Let's open the last gift. Could this be God's special gift to you? *(Picture of Jesus with child.) (Have child open gift.)* While Carmen is opening up the last package, let's remember what we've learned about God's special Christmas gift. Remember, it's for big boys and big girls and little boys and little girls. And it's always there; you can't eat it up or get rid of it, and it doesn't get rotten.

(Show picture of Jesus.) What is God's special Christmas present to you? Jesus! That's right! Jesus is your special Christmas present from God. And He belongs to Carmen just as much as He belongs to Joey; and He's yours even when you grow up. Jesus is always with you. You can't get rid of Him. He doesn't get rotten. And do you know what's the best thing of all? He's strong. He's powerful. He also wants to help you in everything you do. Isn't He a perfect present?

Did you thank God for giving you Jesus this Christmas? Let's thank Him now. Shall we? *(Pray.)*

48
The Three Gifts of the Wise Men

Scripture: Matthew 2:11.

Objects: Picture of the wise men; three gifts; pictures of child praying, child fighting, happy child; picture of Jesus on the cross.

Preparation: Wrap the gifts very beautifully. For gift of gold use a gold colored chest or wrap a box in gold foil; for gift of frankincense use a flower fragrance spray perfume; and for myrrh use a jar of spice-scented cream perfume.

Introduction for Parents and Friends: Mothers, fathers, and friends, Christmas is a wonderful time of the year to make lasting impressions. Perhaps our lesson today, found in Matthew 2:11, will help you to relate to this season more significantly.

Sermonette:

Can anybody guess what our story is about today? That's right. The gifts of the three wise men. Who did the wise men bring their gifts to? Jesus. Do you suppose Jesus still likes gifts? Yes!

This morning we're going to pretend that we are the three wise men. Let's see what gifts we can bring to Jesus. This is the gift the first wise man brought. *(**Hold up first gift of gold.**)* Do you remember what it was?

(Let child open it.) Gold! Gold is very precious and very valuable. Can you bring Jesus gold today? Yes. Jesus says that your faith is like gold, tried in the fire and made pure. *(Show picture of child praying.)* Faith is trusting Jesus. This morning you can bring Jesus the gift of gold and trust Him.

What was the gift the second wise man brought? Frankincense. *(Let child open second gift.)* Frankincense is the perfume of flowers. *(Spray the perfume.)* Doesn't that smell good? You know, Jesus had the inside of His special tabernacle-tent and temple-church filled with the smell of frankincense so that when the priest came out of the temple everybody could smell that he had been in Jesus' temple. Do you think you can bring Jesus the gift of frankincense today? We're told that everybody has an atmosphere of influence that surrounds them. When we have spent time with Jesus, our influence is like the smell of frankincense. Everybody can tell it because we're kind and thoughtful and helpful. I have two pictures here, and just by looking, I'm sure that you can tell which one would smell like frankincense. *(Show pictures of happy child and fighting child.)* Today if you make time to spend with Jesus, you can bring Jesus the gift of frankincense and have a happy, loving, thoughtful influence around you.

Now, what's the gift that the third wise man brought to Jesus? Myrrh. *(Let child unwrap third gift.)* Myrrh is the special perfume of spices. In Jesus' time, myrrh was used mostly to anoint the dead. When Jesus died, Nicodemus brought myrrh to put all over Jesus' body. Do you think that you could bring Jesus the gift of myrrh this morning? Do you think Jesus would want something dead? Yes, there is one thing that Jesus wants dead, and that is self—selfishness. Selfishness is doing what we want to do instead of doing what Jesus would want us to do. Selfishness means doing it our own way instead of Jesus' way. Remember *(Show picture of cross)* even Jesus had to kill self and selfishness. In the garden before

He was killed, remember how He prayed. "God in heaven, I don't want to die on that cross! I don't want to! I don't want to!" He said it three times. But then what else did He say? "But I'll do what You want Me to, even if it means dying!" Boys and girls, you *can* bring Jesus the gift of myrrh this morning, by telling Jesus, "I don't want to do it Your way, I really don't want to do what You want me to, BUT, I'll do it Your way anyway." That's crucifying self and making selfishness dead.

Now, do you remember how we can bring the gifts of the wise men? The first gift was gold, and that is trusting Jesus no matter what. *(Put praying child next to gold chest.)* The second gift was frankincense, and that is making time to be with Jesus so everybody around you can "smell" that you've been with Him. *(Put happy child next to spray perfume.)* And the third gift was myrrh, and that is having self dead so that you can say, "Not what I want, but what You want, Jesus." *(Put picture of cross next to cream.)*

This Christmas, let's bring Jesus these three gifts like the wise men of old did.

Alphabetical Index

(Numbers after entries refer to the numbers of the story, not the page number.)

Aloe vera plant 3
Appearance
  doesn't determine value 12, 32, 37
  not index of inner beauty 16
Atmosphere, around person 2
Attractions, worldy 10
Beauty, outward only 37
Bible
  as aloe vera 3
  as collection of jewels 4
  as milk 20
  as mirror 8
  as rough surface 25
  our instructions 43
  study of 3, 8
Body parts, members of church 19
Campfire 25
Carefulness in little jobs 24
Cares of life 30
Character development 9, 26
  bad traits take over 28
  Christ perfects 28
  defects 28

deformed 26
pattern needed 43
Death, inner without Jesus 37
Deeds, good 1
Discipline 9
Discouragement 21, 22, 29
Dressing appropriately 31
Encouragement, how to give effective 29
Face
  angry 8
  dirty 8, 27
Faith
  as a match 6
  given to each person 6
  must be used 6
Families, work as a unit 18
Frankincense, our witness 48,
Friend
  being effective 29
  how to choose 12
Garden, like our characters 9
Gold, trust in Jesus 48
Growth, depends on milk 20
Heart, giving it to Jesus 45
Heaven, being ready for 21
Idolatry 36
Influence 2
Instruction, listening 32
Irritations 13
Jesus
  as a magnet 29
  as water of life 13, 27, 31
  concern for you 38
  connection with 25
  develop relationship with 7
  died to self 48
  gives new mind 45
  gives us light 39

God's special gift to us 47
looks on heart 12
lovely person 7
more powerful than Satan 35
needs each person 11
our happiness, kindness, obedience 35
perfect gift 47
receives Satan's bite for us 34
strength to do good deeds 1
turns troubles into jewels 17
Way, the 21, 25
Jewels 4
Jobs, importance of little 24
Junk 10
Leaders, showing respect to 14
Leprosy, curse for criticizing 15
Life, emptied of self 10
Light
Christmas 46
from Jesus 39
from using faith 6
Lily of the valley 7
Lips, a sacrifice 44
Lives, changed 21
Love, filled with Jesus' 10
Murmuring 17
Myrrh, death to self 48
Nature, book of 26
Offerings 45
Parents, as God to children 36
Perfection, only in Jesus 5
Perfume 2
Pilgrims 45
Pins 4
Promise
how to claim 3
kept away by unbelief 13
Rebellion 36

Responsibility, as family member 18
Rose of Sharon 7
Sabbath School, importance of 20
Sacrifice 44
Satan
  as a snake 34
  makes us fall 35
Self
  death to 30
  must be emptied 1
Shapes 38
Sharing 45
Size, not important 11
Stubbornness 36
Thanksgiving 44, 45
Trials 22
Troubles 17
Trust in Jesus 5, 26, 35
Unbelief, keeps promises away 13
Washing dishes 33
Water, represents Jesus 13, 27, 31, 33
Weed, bad character trait 9
Wise men, brought significant gifts 48
Words, reveal state of mind 16
Work, together 18

Subject Index

(Numbers after the entries refer to the number of the story, not the page number.)

THE BIBLE
  Study, promises, value 3, 4, 8, 13, 14, 25

CHARACTER DEVELOPMENT
  Accepting trouble 17, 22
  Being content with present duties 24
  Character development 9, 26, 28, 36, 43
  Outward beauty not index 12, 16, 37
  Sabbath School for Christian growth 20
  Self must be emptied 1, 10

CHRIST
  Beauty of 7, 39
  Connection with 25, 34, 39
  Power, living in me 1, 5, 35, 37
  Way and council 13, 26, 30, 32

CHRISTIAN DOCTRINE
  Faith 5, 6
  Justification 1, 23, 27, 28, 29, 30, 31, 33, 34, 35, 37, 40
  New birth 30
  Perfection 5, 31
  Sanctification 21, 26, 31, 33, 39

HOLIDAYS
Christmas 46, 47, 48
New Year 43
Thanksgiving 44, 45

INTERPERSONAL RELATIONSHIPS
Criticizing leadership 15
Effective friendship 29
Everybody's important 11, 18, 19, 38
Family 14, 18
Witnessing 2, 29

Index by Objects

(Numbers after the entries refer to the number of the story, not the page number.)

Aloe vera, leaf 3
Aluminum foil 25
Baby, newborn 20
Bag
  paper 33, 37
  plastic 32
Baskets 11, 28, 36, 45
Beans 22
Bible 3, 4, 21, 24, 25, 42
Bicycle
  hand grips, rubber 42
  handlebar 42
  manual for assembly 42
Blackboard 38
  chalk 38
Blossoms (see Flowers)
Blouse, dirty 31
Bones, dry 37
Bottle, baby 20
Bouquet of flowers (see Flowers)
    Boxes
  chest, gold 48
  crate, for fruit 28
  small, with lid 29

Butterfly 30
Candle 21
Cardboard 13, 44
  heart shape 45
Caterpillar 30
Chalk (see Blackboard)
Christmas
  balls 46
  gifts 47, 48
  lights 46
  ornaments 46
  tree 46
Cocoon (chrysalis)
  empty 30
  full 30
Coral pieces 18
Corn on the cob (see Vegetables)
Cotton 1
Crate, for fruit (see Boxes)
Cutting board 12
Dirt clods 8, 16, 27
Dishes, dirty 33
Doll, large paper 19
Facecloth 8, 27
Flannelboard 14
Flowers 7
  blossoms 24
  bouquet of 10
Fruit (mangos, apples or other) 12, 45, 47
  orange 34
  peaches 28
Funnel 21
Glasses, drinking 13, 16
Globe, of world 39
Gloves, white 1
Hazelnuts 22
Hand grips (see Bicycle)
Handlebars (see Bicycle)

Ice 41
Idol 36
Jar 22, 31
Kettle 11
Kindling 25
Knife 3, 12
Lantern 6
Magnet 29
Manual for assembly (see Bicycle)
Match 6, 21
Matchbox 25
Measuring cups, set 11
Mirror 8
Oyster shell 17
Pan 23, 41
Paper, slips of 13
   (see Doll also)
Pattern 43
Pearl 17
Perfume
   cream 48
   spray 2, 48
Pica pica vine 32
Pictures
   altar with lamb 44, 45
   camp of Israel 14
   cemetery 37
   child
      fighting 48
      happy 48
      praying 48
   cloud of presence 15
   coral polyps 18
   crown jewels 4
   dress, party 31
   faces
   angry 27
   mean 27

   family 14, 18
      food, plate of 33
   garden 9
   idol worshipers 36
   Jesus
     on cross 48
     with children 37, 47
   lady, old 15
   lawn, green 37
   moon 39
   penguins 41
   Pilgrims 44, 45
   Satan 34
   Saul and witch 36
   snake, mamba 34
   spiders 35
     spinnerets 35
     web 35
   tabernacle 15
   vegetables 9
   wise men, three 48
Pins 4
Pitcher
  glass 33
  silver 16
Plant, dying 13
Plant food 2
Potatoes (see Vegetables)
Pots 23
Scissors 19, 43
Screws 29
Seed pods 26
Shells 38
Shirt 47
Spoon, large 16
Spotlight 39
Squash seeds 40
Stone 17

Surgical mask 24
Tabernacle with cloud (flannel) 14
Thermos 42
Tray 11, 16, 33
Trumpet 14
Vases 10, 11
Vegetables 45
   corn on the cob 25
   potatoes 25
   squash seed 40
Water 13, 16, 27, 31, 33, 41, 42
Weeds 9
Yardage 43

Scripture Index

(Numbers after the entries refer to the number of the story, not the page number.)

1 Samuel 15:22, 23	36
1 Samuel 16:7	12
1 Chronicles 28:9	28
Job 8:13, 14	35
Psalm 55:16, 17	23
Psalm 91:14, 15	34
Psalm 118:8	35
Psalm 119:105	42
Psalm 139:14	38
Psalm 139:23, 24	28
Proverbs 8:33	32
Proverbs 29:15	9
Song of Solomon 2:1	7
Isaiah 55:8, 9	21
Isaiah 59:1, 2	13
Jeremiah 2:13	31
Matthew 2:11	48
Matthew 5:14	46
Matthew 5:14, 16	25
Matthew 12:34, 35	16
Matthew 13:44	4
Matthew 25:40	45
Mark 4:30-32	40
Luke 11:44	37

John 3:16	47
John 4:10	33
John 15:15	29
Acts 4:13	2
Romans 8:28	17
Romans 12:3	6
Romans 12:4, 5	19
Romans 14:17	40
1 Corinthians 1:30, 31	5
1 Corinthians 10:11, 12	14
1 Corinthians 10:13	41
2 Corinthians 4:3, 4	39
2 Corinthians 5:17	30
Galatians 2:20	1
Ephesians 3:17-19	10
Colossians 3:18-21	18
Colossians 3:23	24
2 Timothy 2:20, 21	11
Hebrews 12:1, 2	26
Hebrews 13:15	44
James 1:23, 24	8
James 4:11	15
1 Peter 2:2	20
1 Peter 2:9	22
1 Peter 2:21	43
2 Peter 1:4	3
1 John 5:4	6
Revelation 21:6	27